SKYWRITING BY WORD OF MOUTH

at last he could see the mountains

SKYWRITING BY WORD OF MOUTH

And Other Writings, Including

THE BALLAD OF JOHN AND YOKO

JOHN LENNON

HARPER & ROW, PUBLISHERS, New York
Cambridge, Philadelphia, San Francisco, Washington
London, Mexico City, São Paulo, Singapore, Sydney

FIRST EDITION

Designed by Lydia Link

Library of Congress Cataloging-in-Publication Data

Lennon, John, 1940–1980
    Skywriting by word of mouth, and other short works, including The Ballad of John and Yoko.

    I. Title.
PR6062.E6S58   1986   823'.914   86-45312
ISBN 0-06-015656-2
ISBN 0-06-015676-7 (limited)

---

86 87 88 89 90 RRD 10 9 8 7 6 5 4 3 2 1

Contents

Contents

Contents

THE
BALLAD
OF
JOHN
AND
YOKO

I'D always had a fantasy about a woman who would be a beautiful, intelligent, dark-haired, high-cheek-boned, free-spirited artist (à la Juliette Greco).

My soul mate.

Someone that I had already known, but somehow had lost.

After a short visit to India on my way home from Australia, the image changed slightly—she had to be a dark-eyed *Oriental*. Naturally, the dream couldn't come true until I had completed the picture.

Now it was complete.

Of course as a teenager, my sexual fantasies were full of Anita Ekberg and the usual giant Nordic goddesses. That is, until Brigitte Bardot became the "love of my life" in the late Fifties. All my girlfriends who weren't dark-haired suffered under my constant pressure to become Brigitte. By the time I married my first wife (who was, I think, a natural auburn), she too had become a long-haired blonde with the obligatory bangs.

Met the real Brigitte a few years later. I was on acid and she was on her way out.

≪ ≫

I finally met Yoko and the dream became a reality.

The only woman I'd ever met who was my equal in every way imaginable. My better, actually. Although I'd had numerous interesting "affairs" in my previous incarnation, I'd never met anyone worth breaking up a happily-married state of boredom for.

Escape, at last! Someone to leave home for! *Somewhere to go.* I'd waited an eternity.

≪ ≫

Since I was extraordinarily shy (especially around beautiful women), my daydreams necessitated that she be aggressive enough to "save me," i.e., "take me away from all this." Yoko, although shy herself, picked up my spirits enough to give me the courage to get the hell out, just in time for me to avoid having to live with my ex-wife's new nose. She also had had side-interests, much to the surprise of my pre-liberated male ego.

They got the new nose. And I got my dream woman. Yoko.

Having been brought up in the genteel poverty of a lower-middle-class environment, I should not have been surprised by the outpouring of race-hatred and anti-female malice to which we were subjected in that bastion of democracy, Great Britain (including the now-reformed Michael Caine, who said something through his cute Cockney lisp to the effect that "I can't see why 'ee don't find a nice English girl"). What a riot! One of "our boys" leaving his Anglo-Saxon (whatever that is) hearth and home and taking up with a bloody Jap to boot! Doesn't he know about *The Bridge on the River Kwai?* Doesn't he remember Pearl Harbour!

The English press had a field day venting all their pent-up hatred of foreigners on Yoko. It must have been hard for them: what with the Common Market and all, they'd had to lay off hating frogs, wogs, clogs, krauts, and eye-ties (in print, that is), not to mention the jungle bunnies. It was humiliating and painful for both of us to have her described as ugly and yellow and other derogatory garbage, especially by a bunch of beer-bellied, red-necked "aging" hacks; you are what you eat and think. We know what they eat and are told what to think: their masters' leftovers.

It was hard for Yoko to understand, having been recognized all her life as one of the most beautiful and intelligent women in Japan. The racism and sexism were overt. I was ashamed of Britain. Even though I was full of race and anti-female prejudice myself (buried deep where it had been planted), I still bought that English fairy story about the Yanks being the racists: "Not us, old boy, it just wouldn't be cricket." The "Gentleman's Agreement" runs from top to bottom. But I must say I've found on my travels that every race thinks it's superior to every other; the same with class (the American myth being they have no class system).

It was a horrifying experience. I thought of asking Johnny Dankworth and Cleo Lane for advice, but never did (they were the only other biracial couple I'd heard of in Britain). The press led the howling mob, and the foul-mouthed Silent Majority followed suit. The hate mail from the cranks was particularly inspiring; I tried to publish it at Jonathan Cape but they thought . . . Still, it made a change from the begging letters which always coincided with whatever well-publicized particular problems we were facing at the moment, e.g.,

I'm sorry to hear of your wife's recent miscarriage. We, too, have suffered the same tragedy as you, sir, but unlike your good selves do not have the wherewithal to purchase a nice semidetached in the south of France, and as you have so much money, you would be making a 100-year-old spastic and his deaf wife and little crippled children very happy. Sir, it's not too much to ask, . . . etc.

Or:

I, too, was planted and wrongfully arrested by the world-renowned British police [another myth down the drain], and also recently narrowly escaped death in a car crash in Scotland,

and wondered if you could see your way to helping a blind priest and his invalid mother get to church on Sundays . . . etc., etc., etc.

And was Jerusalem builded there? I doubt it.

Apart from giving me the courage to break out of the Stockbroker Belt . . . Yoko also gave me the inner strength to look more closely at my other marriage. *My real marriage.* To the Beatles, which was more stifling than my domestic life. Although I had thought of it often enough, I lacked the guts to make the break earlier.

My life with the Beatles had become a trap. A tape loop. I had made previous short excursions on my own, writing books, helping convert them into a play for the National Theatre. I'd even made a movie without the others (a lousy one at that, directed by that zany man in search of power, Dick Lester). But I had made the movie more in reaction to the fact that the Beatles had decided to stop touring than with real independence in mind. Although even then (1965) my eye was already on freedom.

Basically, I was panicked by the idea of having "nothing to do." What is life, without touring? Life, that's what. I always remember to thank Jesus for the end of my touring days; if I hadn't said that the Beatles were "bigger than Jesus" and upset the very Christian

Ku Klux Klan, well, Lord, I might still be up there with all the other performing fleas! God bless America. Thank you, Jesus.

When I finally had the guts to tell the other three that I, quote, wanted a divorce, unquote, they knew it was for real, unlike Ringo and George's previous threats to leave. I must say I felt guilty for springing it on them at such short notice. After all, I had Yoko—they only had each other. I was guilty enough to give McCartney credit as a co-writer on my first independent single instead of giving it to Yoko, who had actually co-authored it ("Give Peace a Chance").

I started the band. I disbanded it. It's as simple as that. Yoko and I instinctively decided that the best form of defense was attack—but in our own sweet way: *Two Virgins,* our first LP, in which the sight of two slightly overweight ex-junkies in the nude gave John and Yoko a damned good laugh and apoplexy to the Philistines of the so-called civilized world! Including those famous avant-garde revolutionary thinkers, Paul, George and It's Only Ringo. I bear them no ill will. In retrospect, the Beatles were no more an important part of my life than any other (and less than some).

It's irrelevant to me whether I ever record again. I started with rock and roll and ended with pure rock and roll (my *Rock and Roll* album). If the urge ever comes over me and it is irresistible, then I will do it for fun. But otherwise I'd just as soon leave well enough alone. I have never subscribed to the view that artists "owe a debt to the public" any more than youth owes its life to king and country. I made myself what I am today. Good and bad. The responsibility is mine alone.

All roads lead to Rome. I opened a shop; the public bought the goods at fair market value. No big deal. And as for show biz, it was never my life. I often wish, knowing it's futile, that Yoko and I weren't famous and we could have a really private life. But it's spilt milk, or rather blood, and I try not to have regrets and don't intend to waste energy and time in an effort to become anonymous. That's as dumb as becoming famous in the first place.

an apple pie bed.

"ALL WE WERE SAYING
WAS GIVE PEACE
A CHANCE"

OUR next move was the famous "Bed-In" for peace. It had taken us a year of shy courting before the two "free-spirited" artists actually got in bed together. But when we did, we invited the whole world. We knew that we could never get married and hide away on a honeymoon without being hounded by the press, so we decided to put the situation to good use and have a few laughs at the same time. This was to be real "Living Theater."

Who could forget the sight of half the world's press pushing and trampling each other at the door of our bedroom in the vain hope of seeing the Beatle and his nigger doing it for Peace in the Amsterdam Hilton's honeymoon suite? Or the sighs of disappointment when it dawned on them that there was to be no sex and we weren't even naked!

For seven days and nights we made ourselves available (9 in the morning till 9 at night) for photographs and interviews. We allowed the fifth (of Scotch) estate to ask us anything they wished. No holds barred. They came up with zilch; only one or two people out of a few hundred visitors to our bedside had any idea whatsoever what was going on. We filmed them all, of course. But we accomplished what we had set out to do; that is, point them in the direction we wanted them to go, rather than suffer them gladly.

It was no use pretending to have a private life; none of that Mick and Bianca bullshit: having tantrums outside the church after they had invited everyone to the wedding in the first place. Daft, I call it.

We tried to repeat our great success in America, by taking the show to Broadway (the Plaza, actually). But the U.S. government decided that we were too dangerous to have around in a hotel bed, talking about peace. So we took the act to Montreal and broadcast (by radio and TV) across the border. I wonder if they thought of sending G. Gordon "Burn, Baby, Burn!" Liddy after us? Many big egos came to see us there: Al Crapp, Dick Gregory, Tim Leary and Rosemary, Tommy Smothers (all except Crapp sang on "Give Peace a Chance"). Did you ever stop to think that Timothy Leary and Gee. Gordon Liddy are opposite sides of the same coin? Two Micks don't make a WASP.

At the same time whilst we were in Canada, my lithographs of John and Yoko fucking and not fucking were being smuggled across the U.S./Canadian border in trucks (these drawings had been arrested in swinging London). Today, they're available at your local gallery at a hundred bucks for one. The *Two Virgins* album cover sells for two hundred. Life doesn't imitate art; *Life is art* (that's what confuses so many up-and-comings; they're too busy being artists to live).

At that period of our life, people accused us of doing everything for the sake of publicity. Wrong again. Everything we did was publicised anyway. It still is—even though we haven't talked to the press in a number of years. It makes no difference; it seems they can't get along without us. Our press-clipping service, which is world-wide, is full of the most bizarre stories. Amongst my favorites is the one that I've gone bald and become a recluse "locked in my penthouse"—a cross between Elvis Presley, Greta Garbo and Howard Hughes—occasionally making cryptic statements like "I've made my contribution to society and don't intend to work again!" If bringing up a child isn't work, what is?

The reality behind the mystery is simply that we are doing what we want to do. Period.

"GIVE PEACE A CHANCE"

John Lennon
L470

"WE'D ALL LOVE
TO SEE THE
PLAN"

NEXT came our "revolutionary period," which blossomed shortly after we landed in the States for a visit. We never intended to live here permanently (although an English astrologer, Patrick Walker, had foretold that I would leave England for good a year earlier). I had no intention of leaving home, for tax or any other reasons. It just happened that way.

We'd got a bit of a reputation from hanging out with the Cambridge Graduate School of Revolutionaries in the U.K. They made us feel so guilty about not hating everyone who wasn't poor that I even wrote and recorded the rather embarrassing "Power to the People" ten years too late (as the now-famous Hunter "Fear and Loathing for a Living" Thompson pointed out in his Vegas book). We kept the royalties, of course.

Anyway, upon our arrival in the U.S., we were practically met off the plane by the "Mork and Mindy" of the Sixties—Jerry Rubin and Abbie Hoffman—and promptly taken on a tour of New York's "underground," which consisted mainly of David Peel singing about dope in Washington Square Park. Jerry and Abbie: two classic, fun-loving hustlers. I can do without Marx and Jesus.

It took a long time and a lot of good magic to get rid of the stench of our lost virginity, although it was fun meeting all the famous underground heroes (no heroines): Bobby Seale and his merry men; Huey Newton in his very expensive-looking military-style clothes; Rennie Davis and his "You pay for it and I'll organize it"; John Sinclair and his faithful Ann Arbor Brigade; and dear old Allen Ginsberg, who if he wasn't lying on the floor "ohming," was embarrassing the fuck out of everyone he could corner by chanting something he called poetry very loudly in their ears (and out the other).

"WE FOUGHT THE LAW
AND THE LAW
LOST"

THE price of that kind of fun was too high. It was almost five years before our battle with the Nixon government was over (presuming it is over). It was Strom "May He Be Enlightened" Thurmond who cast the first stone; he wrote to the then Attorney General of the United States, John "Take My Wife" Mitchell (they took her; R.I.P. Martha), suggesting that somehow they throw us out of America before the Republican National Convention in San Diego. I understand the reasoning behind the attack, especially after one of our bigmouthed revolutionary heroes had broadcast to the world that John and Yoko were organizing a massed rally to blow away the Republicans at San Diego.

There had been a grand pow-wow at our Bank Street apartment. All the heroes were there. It seemed that without John and Yoko's drawing power, there wasn't going to be a revolution. The Left and Right were both labouring under that illusion. I think Ginsberg was the only one there besides ourselves who thought that the whole idea stunk, and was not only dangerous but stupid. But apparently, the "leaders" of the movement wanted another "Chicago." And we were to be the bait, only we said no. It didn't make much difference, because simply putting out the message through *Rolling Stone* that we *were* coming would convince enough people that we had agreed to it. It convinced Nixon's people.

Mae "They're Coming Through the Windows!" Brussel and Paul Krassner told us that Jerry and Abbie and the whole of the Chicago Seven were double agents for the C.I.A. (except Krassner, of course). We never did find out.

The thing that bothered most of our revolutionary brothers was the fact that we weren't *against* anything, just *for* things, you know, like peace and love and all that naïve crap. That was not macho enough for the tough Jewish Haggendass (not the ice cream). I mean, man, they were the Chicago Seven and *knew the Black Panthers*. Whilst they tried to "use" us, we tried to "convert" them. We even got them on *The Mike Douglas Show,* but none of them knew how to talk to the people —never mind lead them!

The other thing no one liked was the fact that we always insisted on keeping physical and legal control over any film footage which included us in it. John Sinclair threatened to sue us, even after we helped get him out of prison! "It ain't fair, John Sinclair." All in all, we had a few laughs and a lot of drugs.

The bottom line was Nixon's government *vs.* John and Yoko, a few friends, a lot of fans, and a small black psychic from Chicago, introduced to us by Dick "I'll Never Eat Another Thing" Gregory. All of whom we are profoundly grateful to.

So, it was "Bell, Book, and Candle" against Mr. Six Six Six Nixon. Yes, we used magic, prayer, and children to fight the good fight.

ask Ralph.
— On Tuesday
   Should we say to press
'we're not going to San Diego'.

"THE MYSTERIOUS
SMELL OF
ROSES"

THE biggest mistake Yoko and I made in that period was allowing ourselves to become influenced by the male-macho "serious revolutionaries," and their insane ideas about killing people to save them from capitalism and/or communism (depending on your point of view). We should have stuck to our own way of working for peace: bed-ins, billboards, etc. And now here we were, fighting the U.S. government with a lawyer who at first didn't believe that it was a politically-motivated court case (he thought we weren't "that important"), or that the F.B.I. was harassing us with phone taps and the like.

He believed later when his own phone was tapped.

We stopped them when we announced on *The Dick Cavett Show* that they were following us and bugging us. (This was the same show where the liberals got a little upset when I said that I didn't believe in this "overpopulation bullshit." But they weren't as upset as an English audience on a similar show back home where they actually booed and hissed us in a most unpleasant manner

31

for being pacifists, backed up by that famous darling of the "serious" music world, none other than Yehudi "Zometimes You Haft to Kill" Menuhin. He, that rumor has it, records one note at a time!)

In the car the first morning on the way to court, we were both very nervous. We had followed the psychic's instructions carefully: read the right passages in the King James Bible, had put the right verses in our boots, and dowsed our ritually folded handkerchiefs with the magic oil.

From pilgrimages to India with magic Alex Mardas, to what turned out to be a phony miracle worker called Babaji (?), who performed conjuring tricks such as pulling cheap watches with his picture on them "out of nowhere" to a packed house of mainly middle-aged American women (whilst outside the camp, thousands of crippled Indians were selling the same cheap stuff to make a living), we found ourselves living outside of San Francisco in San Mateo in the home of an alcoholic Kung Fu master and acupuncturist and his family. It was he who was responsible for helping us survive methadone withdrawal, which had almost killed Yoko. He also convinced me that my English doctor was wrong (the guy had told me that we could never have babies because I'd blown my sperm with years of misuse of drugs, etc., causing me to have a terrible depression, especially after immigration authorities had revoked my visa in the middle of Art Janov's primal therapy and we had immediately got hooked on smack). Withdrawing cold turkey by taking a boat to Japan from L.A. (similar to a boat trip that Dr. Hong told us he had taken in his youth to get off opium), we arrived in Yokohama, drug-free and happy. It was then that I met Yoko's parents for the first time.

When we recovered from the methadone trip with the good doctor, his good-cooking wife, and helpful daughter, he said, "You want baby? Stop taking drugs, eat good food, in one year you will have it. I promise you." God bless him, he was right. He died without seeing Sean in the flesh, but we did manage to send him a Polaroid I'd taken of the baby when we were still in New York hospital. We are still in touch with the Hongs.

I was talking to Helen (well, at Helen, really), and as usual I found myself on the defensive about "mystics." I didn't get too frantic for a change. Anyway, I found myself saying something like the following—that many, if not all, great men and women were "mystics" in a sense: Einstein, who at the end of his life remarked that if he had to do it over, he would have spent more time on the spiritual; Pythagoras and Newton were mystics. But the main point I was getting at was the fact that in order to receive the "wholly spirit," i.e., creative inspiration (whether you are labelled an artist, scientist, mystic, psychic, etc.), the main "problem" was emptying the mind.

You can't paint a picture on dirty paper; you need a clean sheet.

33

≪ ≫

Van Gogh's "going crazy," Dylan Thomas's "drinking himself to death," etc., were just efforts on their behalf to break out of the straightjacket of their own minds. I include myself and my generation's so-called "drug abuse." Self-abuse would be a more apt expression.

Anyway, I saw the life of Gauguin on TV, and it struck me that he'd died in such a pitiful way (V.D., for which the "cure" was mercury), with a foot broken and twisted from a drunken brawl after returning home for his first "successful" opening in Paris. He had gone to Tahiti to escape his own straightjacket: Working at a bank. A wife and children, one whom he was particularly fond of, a daughter to whom he had been dedicating a personal journal he kept whilst living in the South Pacific, explaining why he had left his family. When he returned to Tahiti, he received a letter from home telling him his daughter had died! What a price to pay to "go down in history." He finally finished his large "masterwork," and died, the point being that, O.K., he was a good painter, but the world could manage quite well without one scrap of his "genius." I believe the "masterwork" was destroyed by fire after his death. The other point being, had he had access to so-called mysticism . . . fasting . . . meditation . . . and other disciplines (as in disciple), he could have reached the "same space." Hard work, I grant you, but easier than killing yourself and those around you.

≪ ≫

It's the same with the Christians (so called). They're so busy condemning themselves and others, or preaching at people, or worse, still killing for Christ. None of them understanding, or trying in the least, to *behave* like a Christ. It seems to me that the only true Christians were (are?) the Gnostics, who believe in self-knowledge, i.e., becoming Christ themselves, reaching the Christ within. Christ, after all, is Greek for *light*.* The Light is the Truth. All any of us are trying to do is precisely that: Turn on the light. All the better to see you with, my

---

* We all recognize that the accepted translation of Christ is "the anointed one." We, however, were told that in the original Dead Sea Scrolls it is revealed that the true translation of Christ is "light," which to us made more sense. —Y.O.L.

dear. Christ, Buddha, Mohammed, Moses, Milarepa, and other great ones spent their time in fasting, praying, meditation, and left "maps" of the territory of "God" for all to see and follow in our own way.

The lesson for me is clear. I've already "lost" one family to produce what? Sgt. Pepper? I am blessed with a second chance. Being a Beatle nearly cost me my life, and certainly cost me a great deal of my health—the drinking and drugs having started before we were professional musicians—all in an effort to reach "out there."

I will not make the same mistake twice in one lifetime. This time around, inspiration will be called down by the ancient methods laid down for all to see.

If I never "produce" anything more for public consumption than "silence," so be it.

Amen.

—1978

TWO
VIRGINS

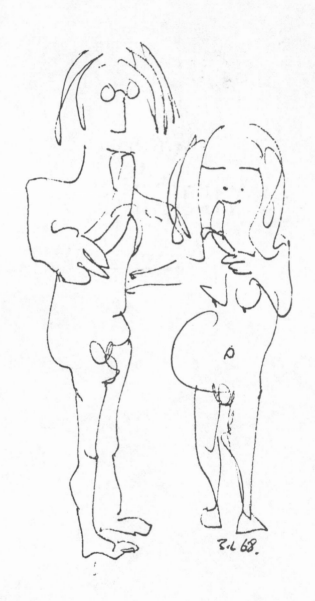

WONSAPONATIME

there was two Balloons called Jock and Yono. They were strictly in love-bound to happen in a million years. They were together man. Unfortunatimetable they both seemed to have previous experience—which kept calling them one way oranother (you know howitis). But they battled on against overwhelming oddities, includo some of there beast friends. Being in love they cloong even the more together man—but some of the poisonessmonster of outrated buslodedshithrowers did stick slightly and they occasionally had to resort to the drycleaners. Luckily this did not kill them and they werent banned from the olympic games. They lived hopefully ever after, and who could blame them.

Once upon a pooltable there limped a short-haired butchers boy by the way of Ostergrad, it comes in sentencesspoolarrow-ick airport. Her father wasisalong story cut short in the middle of his lifesentence. We are indebted to the colloquial orifice for its emediate diposalaronowitz. In concluding i might add hoc virtallo virttutembe. on the other handbag i mean tosay lamouray nous sommes toujourialistic.

ally speaking this film is about an hourglasshouseboat. The full meaning of winchester cathedral defies description. their loss was our gainsboroughnil. the sound of a manservantile defectivelyingbastardonopilisgaverdale time. how close can you getisburgandeviatorycouncilriginaly a birdbath feeling sort of disatisfiedthe founder was a bricklayer. i. theylooked into each others eyeballs their tongue clenched minds grasping at each others whatsits. this was elementary and the beginning of a new line only now it is an old one already —see how it ages be on your very askey . . . known as a briefcase of malaria. to reign over us god save the queen (A HARD WORD) perhaps she is right to say tape it but its not the same is it??? taping is tapingisstapingadpolerotiniouslyaboutaswellasanythingelseon earth do dwell a scarlet little child who is lost to us all in his approach to humaniteatimetable to kepp up with hisownhearse feeling a liiile sick myself.

WITH A CAPITI MY. to whom it may

John Lennon 1968

AN
ALPHABET

———◆———

A is for Parrot which we can plainly see.

B is for glasses which we can plainly see.

C is for plastic which we can plainly see

D is for Doris

E is for binoculars I'll get it in five

F is for Ethel who lives next door

G is for Orange which we love to eat when we can get them because they come from abroad

H is for England and (Heather)

I is for monkey we see in the tree

J is for parrot which we can plainly see

K is for shoetop we wear to the ball

L is for Lamp because lamp

M is for Venezuela where the oranges come from

N is for Brazil near Venezuela (very near)

O is for football which we kick about a bit

T is for Tommy who won the war

Q is a garden which we can plainly see

R is for intestines which hurt when we dance

S is for pancake or whole wheat bread

U is for Ethel who lives on the hill

P is arab and her sister will

V is for me

W is for lighter which never lights

X is easter — have one yourself

Y is a crooked letter and you can't straighten it

Z is for Apple which we can plainly see.

This is my story both humble and true
Take it to pieces and mend it with glue.

                John Lennon 1969. Feb.

A   is for Parrot which we can plainly see

B   is for glasses which we can plainly see

C   is for plastic which we can plainly see

D   is for Doris

E   is for binoculars I'll get it in five

F   is for Ethel who lives next door

G   is for orange which we love to eat when we can get
    them because they come from abroad

H   is for England and (Heather)

I   is for monkey we see in the tree

J   is for parrot which we can plainly see

K   is for shoetop we wear to the ball

L   is for Land because brown

M   is for Venezuela where the oranges come from

N   is for Brazil near Venezuela (very near)

O   is for football which we kick about a bit

T   is for Tommy who won the war

Q   is a garden which we can plainly see

R   is for intestines which hurt when we dance

S   is for pancake or whole-wheat bread

U   is for Ethel who lives on the hill

P   is arab and her sister will

V   is for me

W   is for lighter which never lights

X   is for easter—have one yourself

Y   is a crooked letter and you can't straighten it

Z   is for Apple which we can plainly see

This is my story both humble and true
Take it to pieces and mend it with glue

—1969

SKYWRITING
BY
WORD
OF
MOUTH

SKYWRITING
BY WORD OF MOUTH

A NOVELTY IN 4/4,

in which our hero finds himself, ten years later, older, madder, but definitely CURED. Picketing the heinous hierarchy for custody of his soul (his organ marked accordingly), delivering a counterblow, reviewing the situation at hand whilst wiping the smut from his eye (a form of osmosis).

Pop goes the we/sell.

In other words, descent into the abbess, or:

"let them eat each other!"

≪ ≫

Face to face with yourself (i.e., left to your own devices): Cutworm or fish bait. Let's face it—whatever *it* is. The code word is *foxhole*.

Let's hear it for the eyes! It's time to take a bathos, for whom the bell telephones; the international T.I.T.

Let it be clearly miss understood; I will not stand for it. I might kneel (cut to the Isle of Man) where a manxcat tells no tales.

Decapitation slants your disposition.

Gratis night and the Pips.

The following NIGHT MARE is horse sense:

- if we cut the birthrate down, will there be more space?

- if you can manicure a cat, can you caticure a man?

All these questions will be answered in the next thousand years or so. Don't call me and I won't call you. The U.N. has looked into the problem and is very disappointed. Insomnia was cured by putting people to sleep. As guilty as pudding. Rice to the occasion. The benefit of kneejerk intellectualism is, it keeps you fit.

Always a bridesmaid
never a couplet.

Skywriting for beginners: HIS ROYAL QUAGMIRE OF MONOLOGUE CORDIALLY INVITES YOU TO A READING OF HIS TEACUP IN THE MANHOLE. A RETROSPECTIVE OF HIS COLLECTED EPICENTRES ON THE OUTSTANDING WAITERS OF THE LAST CENTURY. BRING YOUR OWN SAP. PATRIOTISM WILL BE SERVED AFTER DINNER. PLEASE R.S.V.P. (IN ANY KNOWN LANGUAGE) TO THE FOLLOWING ADDRESS:

"Ladies and gentlemen, I give you something to chew on, followed by a short pause. It has been my misfortune to have tangled with the rites of a tree worshiping group of unabashed individualists. This ancient cult who, as the layman would term it, are an interaction between two positive negatives, thereby producing an uncanny resemblance to his majesty the Queen.

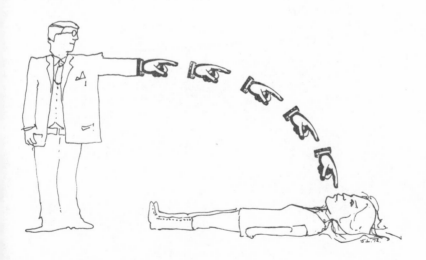

"With this power alone, they can affect all her descendants, not to mention her Children. Even now, as I talk, I can sense a kind of creeping paralysis of Jowl. If we are not strong in our Convictions, our Jails will overflow with these Creatures who have no Respect. On these words I leave you slightly dazed but not defeated, and I thank you."

It never fails to rouse the mob. A fertility cult is etching reindeer on the parched fragments of a twice-forgotten civil airline. Nam June Jersey Turnpike, the famed turniqué of avant-reguarde action, is known to have dabbled. Hypothesis: If the ecumenical council relieves itself of duty, do they clean up?

Indeed, this question was bandied around the RAN-DUM corporation, and it slowly drove them home. Here is their survey, taken at RANDUM itself; you may draw your own cartoons. . . .

SUBTITLED
"LUCY IN THE SCARF
WITH DIABETICS"

. . . it has come to our atissue (bless you), that war is only profitable to those left behind; to wit, if and when the Third World War (most aptly titled) breaks out, who will know who won? We at RANDUM have a lot of machines. WHO WILL RUN THEM?

The late President Exxon was himself heard to mumble "Hurt me! hurt me!" but his democracy was never taped. His Matron was seen to test his cocoa for signs of the times, such as Communist footballs or deliberate nutshells on the White House lawn. (One such was found in the Garden of Unaccountably Deadly Plants, but it was never proven.) Soon to become a household worm, his name went down thoroughly in history. His library will contain the ashes of every one he knew and the Howard HUGE Memorial Hospital next door will only admit dead people, for fear of Spreading Some Unconscionable Disease. Mr. HUGE himself was a well-known hyperconduit.

Although this study took only four years to garnish, it still smelled a little. Well, the Rabbit Warren Report looked good too, apart from the strange theory that the same bullet killed both John Kennedy and Efrem Zimbalist Jr. without stopping for lunch. The author, a previous Chef of the C.I.A., has spent many long hours in a motel toilet somewhere off the coast of Cubans (also known as Florid, or God's Waiting Room). He would not reveal his sorceress even under the threat of love. He's our kinda guy.

Next week we'll discuss "How to Satisfy a Dead Housewife," a closer look at feminism by the author of "Take My Wife Anywhere," in which J. Walter Tombe-stone investigates himself too closely in front of a group of admirers. This form of Grudge Therapy is catching on like a pleasant disease all across America; many names have appeared at the home of Dr. Grudge in need of help. A reformed member of the F.B.I., he has been tailing himself for fourteen years in an effort to Get At The Truth.

We will continue our six-part serious on the life of seemingly ordinary Peculiarities entitled "I Wonder the Streets of Old New York":

>   ah, the smell of lice squads
>   the half-baked politician
>   his inorganic possibilities displayed
>   all over forty-ninth street
>   in an obvious bid for power.

The winner is stretched in Bloomingdale's window as an example of Western art. Well, that's the way God planned it. I leave you as I found you—only some time later.

UP YOURS

a closer look at feminism
by Deirdre De Flowered, b.s.

THIS romantic-sounding novel is set in the fif-
teenth century, the year of oh Lord! nineteen twenty-
three:

I smoked my way down to the ground floor, still
suffering from a slight case of vernacular. My former
husband (who has never recovered) had hidden himself
in the home of my best friend, Sir Lute Arthrite, one of
the few remaining Arthrites of Lebanon. She was de-
scended from an unbroken line of inquiry reaching back
into the dark recesses of the mind (what she was doing
there I never did find out). I was an unattached case of
terminal entrée when I married my sister's half-brother
just after his operation for urban renewal (a successful
case I might add), when I received my second inkling.

≪ ≫

One thing stood out in my father's bedroom (as
mother used to say, "If it isn't one thing it's another").
I can still see her face as she swept through the dining

room in search of the Nile (Father having worn Arabs'
undies ever since the Bay of Pigs). I was studying a
chemist in the slightly diminished College of Opportu-
nity on a grant handed down through the will of God.
How could I forget my heritage? I'd last seen it at the
housewarming party of the International Brotherhood of
Seamstresses. I'd always suffered from catarrh, but fortunately never had it so good, and it was through this
that I finally caught sight of myself in the mirror.

It was at a séance. The doors were closed (how sym-
bolic). The trumpet danced and the Scottish dance music
was slightly insane. All the same, I got the message.

Since then, I've never looked black. My life has been
guided by an unseen piano player, who is actually typing
this now. It's out of my head, as it were. I asked him
what it was like "beyond the veil"; here is his understate-
ment:

"It's not all that different."

I might have known! But still my burning quest for
matches did not stop. It was to lead me into the most
uncompromising situation:

Lebanon: The air is thick with piss; the sound of
vomiting can be heard for miles. At sundown I face east
and raise my eyebrows to the north (very difficult); a low
moaning comes from the corner of the room. It is as if
time had stood still. It is a camel in pain. He looks
quickly in my direction. I close my eyes and go away.

The next morning nothing remains but a quiet rebuttal from my publisher's editorial staff.

Inexplicable as it may seem to the reader, survival after life is a certainty. I can prove it beyond the shadow of a doubting Thomas. Here are some entrails from my diary:

nine o'clock, Tuesday the eighth: "I saw it again."
Friday the fifth: "Nobody called."
March 27: "Hollow laughter."

A lawyer would be unconvinced, but how do you account for the voices? Only the true adept will understand the deeper significance of what I am about to say:

"The language of flagon is hidden 'neath the fizz of symbolism, which lies 'twixt the cup and lip of unearthly delights." Or, "austere measures must be taken by force."

This comes under the previous heading, "Stealthily Whining Your Way to the Top."

"Bend over. . . . Look at me while I'm speaking. . . . Say after me three times . . ."

Be/deviled by this train of thought, I slowly cut off all communications with my spirit piano player. The last thing I heard was "up yours" to the tune of "Annie Laurie." To this day, I am still looking for a decent-sized apartment in New Jersey for the right price.

A congealed hi!way was the initial instigator. In the face of adversity, the disciples were choked in the foyer. A fraction of their instincts now remain. Modus operator shipping magnet grinds to a halt. Convictions disguise content. Moonlight simmer. Elation upgrading psyche. Erectile projectile. Deranged minor found digging. Upshot of the longshot is a sureshot.

PUMA EATS COAST GUARD

or Genghis Khan Leaves a Vast Impression

PART ONE

The coast guard loses his cool.

IT was a large part of Max's orifices that had served him well during the recent "stagnation." An unqualified success was written all over him during a discourse on the probability of improbability. Max's hair had been a mess. Being a coast guard had its problems. Apart from the virtual isolation, the wind kept ruining his rod stewart. It had taken him six months, more or less, to look like an idiot, and more than fifty dollars (American). He was not too thrilled with the outcome.

Max could not distinguish between a vaginal spray and underarm deodorant. "The problem is," he used to moan, "I don't know which to spray first." These kind of things bore heavily on his mind. (What else did he have to think about just gazing out to sea?) Being very short-sighted and easily led did not help matters. He could not even see the rarely-spotted Qualm, a beauty of a beast that lurks over Iceland. It lets out a blood-curdling but stealthy stream of epitaphs whenever it is disturbed. Which isn't often.

In the fog, which was frequent, he was a friend in need. This pressure was an acrid and pernicious aggravation to his already hampered lifestyle. Apart from that, it was a drag. "My Head is ambushed," he was oft heard to scream from the isolation of his government-subsidised lifeboat. But who would care in the capitalist non-agrarian society he called home? His mother answered the phone. "It's me, Mam," he said in order to clarify the situation. "It's Max." "How are ya, Max, how's ya Head," she would reply in that special voice she reserved for her only begotten son. He called her every Sunday, she called him twice a month. He could picture her in his mind's eye, skewering a frog (she was of French extraction). Probably sucking on its leg right now. He remembered affectionately the way she would spit her teeth into an antique before reaching into the family freezer for the Sunday joint. She was on morphine, and had been for the past fifteen years. "I'm immune," she would chant as she ran headlong into the bitter Atlantic wearing nothing but a wig, "I'm one of God's own!"

This was to become deeply ingrained in the very being of Max at quite an early age, really (not to mention her wrestling with authority every other month. The winner got to wear a three-ply rope, fashioned after the style of Hemingway). "That's what toughens the instep," she repeatedly told him. "Only by diligently practicing the art will you ever become *half* the man your mother is," she would warn, with a playful smack about the head of the slowly-receding Max. It was not till many years later that Max was to learn of the impending doom prophesied in her extraordinary procrastinations.

≪ ≫

Max's father had died at an inconvenient age, leaving inconclusive evidence. Holiness comes slowly to a man of means. It was an anachronism to his purulence which led to a judgment being brought against him "and all his team" in a court case which was to shock the America of the Sixties, reaching saturation point during the "red scare" tactics encouraged by a completely deaf chief of police who had spent his formative years arresting "would-be ice skaters" off the coast of Maine.

To expedite matters, the renowned police chief, known to his friends and enemies alike as Frizby, had encouraged Max to dabble in what was later to be referred to as "soft-core Puritanism." The Cardinals of this movement apparently rose to power by rubbing two sticks together, thus producing sawdust (to the amazement of all concerned). This was then sprinkled over the homes of "non-believers" in the hopes that it would leave a lasting impression. No one remembers the good thing, but that's life. Neoplasm was no barrier to a man versed in pumice stone. "Think of all the teeth you're cleaning," Max told himself. "Think of your erroneous surroundings." "Think of yourself!" his aged mother nagged. "Think of yourself or be damned!"

His fiery first wife had arrived on an installment plan, via Texas, but Max had not read the penalty clause too closely. She was an expansive freemason and the proud daughter of a street salesman. She was courteous, curious, and starving. This led to a long and difficult pregnancy, but the child was born a healthy and bouncing baby (with the help of a large bottle of vodka). Clarissa came into the world with a "hell of a laugh." It seems like only yesterday.

One of my earliest recollections is of seeing the whole damn family clubbing oysters to death in their vegetable garden. But the Depression soon put a stop to that. Now, they had only each other. Clarissa was later drowned chasing sewer rats for the school. Max never recovered. From then on, his heart just wasn't in it. Of course he carried on watching seagulls, but everyone knew instinctively that "wall-eyed look" was here to stay. He also gave up conniving.

Who knows to what heights this man might have gone if it had not been for his vertigo? Anyway, he was eaten by a puma. More on this later.

PUMA EATS SCAPEGOAT

PART TWO
in the continuing saga, in which Max gets to
write his epitaph:
"Eternity Is a Hell of a Long Time"

I have told you of Max's interest in wildlife (oysters, etc.). This was only part of the story. Materialism was his main concern, goldfish coming a close third. He was fond of fruitfulness. This he would eat every morning unusually mixed with a yogurt. His calorie intake was on a par with the growth of his benign stigmoid (later to give him hell).

His day was strictly ritualized. Every morning at six twice round the vegetable garden, followed by a brisk janitor up the bypath to the grief-stricken quicksand half a mile or so from his hut.

This region, known as Saturation Point, was a favorite spot with the tourists in summer. A dramatic landscape indeed, with its pounding surfers and convoluted gallop polls. Atop a small chalk cliff one could see across to Martha's Graveyard, home of the Quackers, a slightly balmy group, known only by a loud moaning on Easter Sunday (the rest of the year they kept pretty much to themselves).

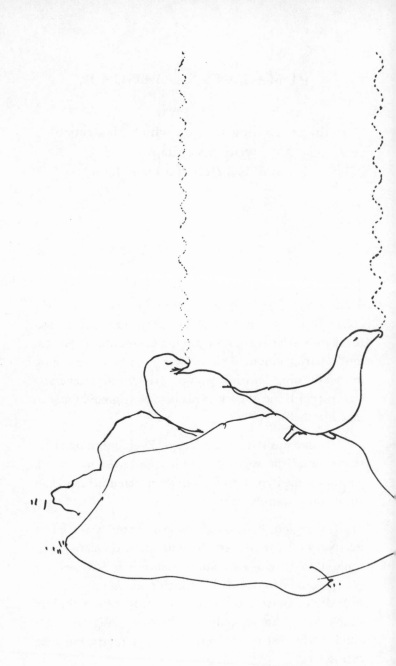

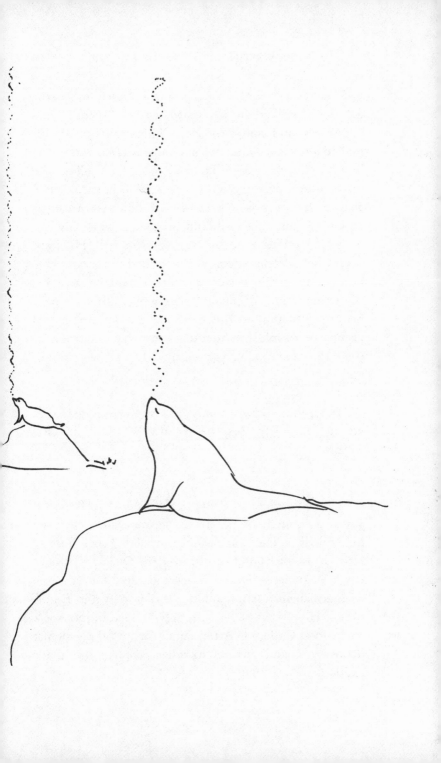

The Emperor of Cowling was rumored to be the founder of the group; he was known for his frothiness, gawkiness, and complete lack of homosexuality. At his funeral a tell-tail Pelise de Foi Gras was eaten with gusto by his followers, whom, however, would not follow him to the grave, even though it was written in the original charter. A cookbook was distributed, followed by constipation. A cantilever was constructed in which the remains of his head were said to be smiling still. His teeth became a collector's item, and were said to contain "certain fillings," the power of which definitely "boggled the imagination." Condominions were built to honour his crumpet and, to this day, you can see single-filed groups of people heading that way, the smartness of their mentality being outmoded only by their strongarm tactics.

A legend, surpassed only by a slight feeling of déjà vu, or jumpiness. In other words, WORDS FAILED THEM.

"Prisoner Held in Contempt of Court by Hysterical Juror" screamed the headline. "Japanese Man Searched for Malady." This did nothing to allay Max's fears of retribution for having turned over the Quackers' files to the local police. "They'll knack my vapor for this," he told a disbelieving prejudge, "this is only the beginning." How right he was can only be seen in retrospect at the local Gallery D'Arter, famed for its "impressionist doorman," and "pictures of other people." But that's another story.

A navigator's tunic was found hidden behind a deeply-carved Fallout Shelter, which Max's mother had installed in her only forgotten son's bedroom. "Mitigating Circumstances Can Be Irritating" was inscribed over the doorway (hand-embroidered at that). A demure backdrop was carefully fickled (tightrope fashion) across the whole episode, leaving speculation to run amok among the tightly-knit community. Certain parties were held, though a lack of waitresses was evident.

In spite of all this, nothing deterred Max in his never-ending search, but nothing was to match the "bloodstained adolescence" of the Lodge, itself a party to the proceedings. "We Will Uphold That Which Is to Be Upheld" was added to the original doctrine some five years after the burial of the Emperor Founder. It was known as *Cowling's Second Coming,* a "Sex Change for Beginners."

It turned out to be one of their more profitable ventures; indeed habitats were outmoded, virtually paupered; slowly but sourly, a deep and abiding impression was manifest; it straddled the populous with its Neanderthal yearnings, but it did not interfear with Max's third (and last) wife.

Melissa, a tall, dark-haired hybrid, winner of two scholarships on "bedwetting in early Rome"; her mind was in brisk contrast to Max's laisser fairground, a job he held in spite of himself (urgent silt required, four days a week, no experience necessary). Max was straight out of college and bent on becoming. Melissa coordinated his symptoms immediately. She had him taped.

He often complained of being "tied down" and "over-crowded." Melissa would have none of his ravings.

She'd married him for better or for worse, and she was about to make the worst of it. "I've earned it, Max," she'd tell him, "I've earned the right to your frontage." This would drive him into a frenzy of correspondence; but what could he do? For what she lacked in passion, she made up for in gardening. "I love to stick my fingers in it, Max," she martyred. "Sometimes I touch worms." Max was in trouble and he knew it, but still his passion

squares.

for her never abated. "Just let me SEE IT!" he begged regularly. "I won't even TOUCH," and with tears in her eyes Melissa would kick him out of the bedroom. "Give me time, Max, just give me a little more time. . . ."

Two years were to pass, very slowly, before Max got a glimpse of her glands. "My god, they're beautiful, Melissa," he gasped. "They're Bigger Than Mommy's!" With a look in her eye that spoke of nothing in particular, Melissa would casually display herself to a small audience. "Thank you, Max, you'll never know how much I appreciate your kindness unless, of course, you ask." He never had the nerve, poor Max, a sloth before his time. His eyesight slowly failing, he was to see less and less of her as the years went by, until one cold and damp morning in September she escaped with an underdeveloped Parkkeeper to live the life "she knew she must!" And as subsequent events were to show, she maintained a quiet dignitary in South Carolina, with a small but interesting clientele. Nothing more was heard from her until the outbreak of hostilities.

SPARE ME THE AGONY OF
YOUR BIRTH CONTROL

CHAPTER IX

UNDERNEATH a small Greek in the
Outer Hebrides, a burning desire was slowly kindling.
"Aos! Aos!" the good Samaritan (a recently retired staff
member of a now defunct Colonel in the Greek Navy)
wrote in strictest confidence (*Aos!* being the subtitle to a
new novel he, Flatima de Ecuador von Knilescope, was
currently in the habit of writing). He signed off with his
customary E.E.K.! That should keep them off the scent,
he thought.

Now to the business at hand: A barbaric heroin trade
between the Greek islands and Turkistan, formally
known as Constantinople. A fish tycoon had been the
instigator. With his massive arms, legs, and a fleet of
fishing boots, it had been a simple process to demystify
the opium seed as it arrived in a puff of smoke off the
Marseilles coast. The code word C.O.D. was tattooed on
the elbow of every member of the international ring of
criminals, known collectively as Trash.

Inspectre Vogue had been on the job for much less
pay than he had imagined, and for twice as many years.

He hated the "criminal element" with a vengeance bordering on discipline, carefully concealed behind a Fisherman's D'warf. "These parasites must be harassed, until they know the full meaning of consistency, and every last drop has been drained from their never-satisfied conglomerate," he paused, "and furthermore, to be continued."

She pulled his scarf more tightly round her neck and headed for the Metro. "Even in this weather a man knows no bounds." He relit his pipe, and vanished in a rather pleasing way. Had he known that right behind him a small northeasterly widow was definitely furnishing his room, he might not have cast aspersions so disparately. How was he to know, with his head in the clouds and his daughter at school? No adjectives could describe his animalism, or his esprice de Corps.

He looked down at his magnified body slowly rippling his spasms. Out of the corner of his third eye he could see the Mediterranean. It was filled with water. Laughing children dipped their parents' personal belongings, willy-nilly, in the briny froth. An air of aboding hung heavy round his lunch. An attractive blonde in a four-piece swimsuit was drowning a little further down the coast; but his mind was on the job. "This would be a holiday if I wasn't working," he told himself over and over, in the way he had been trained. He could never forget the fun he'd had bringing the children to this very same spot to learn to drown. How could he? He was still a young man in his early forties, slightly balding, but none the worse for weapons.

He'd been schooled in the art of De Bauchery, long, endless nights of physical laughter in the mountains of Sicily. An outlaw by profession, an inlaw by marriage. His tail lights were deteriorating, but his collection of porcelain remained a constant companion.

A short term in prison had served to harden his arteries. He was understaffed, and feeling the pinch. His geopolitical thoroughness covered a multitude of sin-bads. As soon as a speech impediment was cured, his word was law. When he gave an order, nobody could keep a straight face. He was called to the Bar frequently to solve various unknown and unsolved murders. "Put Inspectre Vogue on the job and you might as well forget it." This and the kitsch Lorraine were amongst his formidable credentials.

He had taken the case with an air of dismay, clouded only by rancid fear, a problem he'd been wrestling with since studying at the Classical Musak College of Inferior Decorating. Having passed the entrance exam with flying hormones, he was never to fulfill his earlier promise due to an oversight on behalf of the Creator. Now he faced the last half of his life with nothing under his belt but his stomach.

A blatant depot in the corner of his mind served only to remind him of his bob cummings. He had a roof over his head, even when he was outdoors. A remarkable man in anyone's book, especially mine! He was adjusting to his outbursts and coming along nicely, when a chill ran down his pants. "It's all very well wearing rubber, but this is getting me up and down." With these thoughts firmly dribbling through his mind, he caught a cold for Instanbull.

Arriving later the same day, he had himself committed to a local hotel. Carefully searching the room for edible spiders, he sank into a deep sleep, and did not wake till morning. Refreshed and overbearing, he hurried down to a quickstep breakfast prepared by a fauning glory. He headed for the Latin Quarter, riding the back of a native who was not new to him, but still gave him a sense of urgency.

Out of the middle of nowhere he caught a whiff of perfume that reminded him strongly of something he couldn't remember. It was only later that it dawned on him: It was the girl in the shaving cream who had first smelled like that! His mind dwindled on her soft posterity, her robust excess, her formal attire. Remembering the mornings they had spent wrapped in each other's hardware. It was she who had taught him to be cunningless and thereby reaching heights of hitherto unknown orgasms; how to bend and stretch her in an endless parade of soldiers, her hair smouldering softly in his face, her buttocks almost clean in that never to be forgotten sun as it beat down on their completely covered bodies. "Take me," she breathed. "Take me somewhere decent."

His mind snapped back like an elastic gauguin. Be Here Now; hadn't he read those lines somewhere? He rolled the words sensuously round his tongue, as if it were some kind of sandwich. The next thing he knew he woke up in a hospital bed. He'd walked under a government agent's diplomatic immunity and lost sight of one arm. "Take it in your stride," he whispered. . . . Was he alone? . . . Or was that a premonition at his feet? He reached for a nurse and screamed. . . .

He slept fitfully. Could he send a message via kaleiderscope? Did he have to dial nine? Was he being held against his will, or did he like it? His mind raced for a taxi.

"DEMENTED IN DENMARK"

HIS trial was set in stone on the outskirts of Nice. His lawyer was a woman well versed in the rationale of poverty. Her appearance belied her size. It awed the judge and disturbed the jury. With this in mind he pleaded for help. Apart from a small group of whole-sailors, which unnerved him somewhat, he was more than happy with his backlot. A thrush fell over the courtroom, you could have heard a pinhead. Nothing disturbed the troubled breathing of the judge. "The witness will rise to the occasion. The rest of you may sit."

A hammer was handed to the judge, and the court reporter was given a mirror. The prosecutor rises suspiciously. His head turns; suddenly his eyes alight on Vogue, who by now is praying feverishly for guidance.

"Our father who ought to hear me . . ." His head pounding, he lifts his pain-wracked counselor.

"Having been duly sworn at, resume the headstand, bare your testicles, and get on with it."

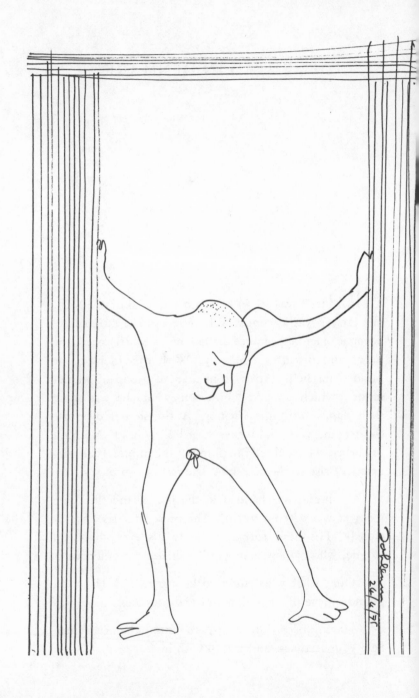

MR. GOTTGRIEFF: I would like to, at the beginning, go through the previous witness's pantsuit; if I may be so bold, your swordship, I would hasten to add, no prejudice in as much, etc., etc., but I do find it difficult to breathe. Perhaps we could open the Plaintiff's mind?

MS. HULKBURT: Objection, m'lud. He's already been wiped by our antecedents.

JUDGE HARDCORP: Objection undermined.

Q: Inspectre Vogue, I would like you to look over my shoulder that has been marked Exhibitionist 256. Do you know where they came from?

A: Do you know where Mr. Hamilton got them?

MS. HULKBURT: Nor does Mr. Wicketbasket.

MR. GOTTGRIEFF: I ask that the following two policemen be marked savagely as the next two exhibitionists in order. Also I ask that a document be admitted to the Bar, dated the 1st day of October 1962, between a few Greeks and Isobel Norman Vogue known previously as In Vogue, a.k.a. Inspectre Vogue.

MS. HULKBURT: I have placed a small partridge in front of the witness.

A: What is this?

Q: Exhibit 256 is the affidavid that was submitted to stress under Marshall Law, the First World Warrior.

A: I just read it.

Q: Does that refresh your recollection that matters set therein occurred? Do you recall any of these things?

A: No, it doesn't hurt at all.

Q: Do you recall that Amie Buttress at that meeting said she was going to "look into your throat for signs of decency"?

A: At that meeting?

Q: Yes.

A: Which meeting was that?

Q: Do you recall anything that Buttress said, apart from "damn you"?

A: No, I mean I don't, I've said I don't remember fuck all in particular about that meeting, if, in fact, we ever met.

JUDGE HARDCORP: Speak up, Witness, I'm masturbating.

Q: Where were you during the entire discussion?

A: I don't know. I just remember going along, and the next thing, I was in Sicily.

Judge Hardcorp rises with a sigh of relief, dismisses himself out of hand, and the trial was adjourned.

Meanwhile, back on Long Island, Max Buttress was getting the short end of the stick from his mother Amie, and he loved it. The previous evening Max had discovered a rare box of Ethiopians on the beach. They had been washed ashore by a storm. Wedged firmly between their teeth were some unnecessarily large packets of illegal heroins that Max was duty-bound to apprehend.

"I love a good perpetrator," he said, dodging his mother's phlegm. "I like to dawdle with their vital equipment."

Thereupon he was besieged by invitations from distant relatives, including his father. "Don't say I never give ya' nothing," Amie whined as she nailed him firmly to the deck. "I'm your mother and don't you forget it!" How could he? Her name was tattooed on his throat, and had been since birth. The Ethiopians kneeled in the corner quickly crossing themselves and murmuring "Hail Selassie, Queen of Dogs." No wonder they were nervous.

The distance between two cousins is negligible, but between Max and Oliver it was even stranger. "We'll have a Mongolian, Max," she said, carefully avoiding his glands. "Just touch it, Olly, you *can't* have a baby through your ass." The power of his eloquence swayed her. She reached out from under the Tractor, and slowly took his temperature. "It's Ninety-nine-point-eight, Max," she said, coyly covering herself in credentials. "It looks like an angry Bratwurst." Max was frantic with unequalled velocity, his mind a tasmanian of desperately simmering dualism. "Should I kill her now or after?"

Round and round the demented pair had dwindled on each other, little knowing how near to immaculate inspection their two hot-buttered adolescent bodies had reached, only to be stopped by an unscheduled aboriginal. "Gee, that was close, Max, we almost made a truck stop." Max zipped up and jumped to a conclusion.

He read and reread her first letter to him (the traces of a lingering death still filled his aching nostrils):

Dearheart,

I've been feeding a cold in Central Park and a realm of bliss, rare ultimate, beyond both knower and known, has been following me since 72nd St. My spirit aware, yet unaware, I am mute and jeff. I barter nothing with trader vics, but I love a good cheese salad. . . .

Also enclosed was a newspaper clipping:

SAVE $30,000,000
BY NOT LIVING IN A PENTHOUSE!!!

For only $10 a day you can have a picture of a penthouse, still live in a ghetto, and pretend you're living in a luxury apartment!!! SEND $40. LIVE LIKE A KING.
Offer expires every thirty minutes.

He closed his eyes and fell overboard.

"IT NEARLY HAPPENED
IN ROME"

WAS it only yesterday they had boarded a flight to Rome? It seemed impossible to ascertain, yet somewhere in the back of Laura's head was a toothpick.

They had met over lunch in Tangiers. Apart from a slight feeling of nausea, they were quite compatible. But their marriage was destined for Hong Kong. He was a defrocked accountant, she a corporal in the Marines. The only thing they had in common was a "healthy respect for flags." This was to see them through good times and worse. "The problem is," mused Hans, "not insurmountable." Laura concurred violently. "It's not that so much, Hans," she responded openly, "it's your accursed accounting for everything." This hurt Hans deeply, but he bit his tongue and gargled.

The plane landed with no visible means of support. They hurried through customs, neither one speaking a word as the limousine smoothed its way through the crowd of Spanish onions. The hotel foyer was hot, dusty, and somewhere on the outskirts of Rome. The English desk clerk greeted them with a smirk. "Welcome to

Rigamortis," he snarled, showing a complete set of National Health teeth. "Your room will be ready in slightly under an hour." "Oh Lord," Laura seethed, "I'm dripping." "Cross your legs, dear," Hans volunteered.

Laura said nothing but continued to look after him with disbelief. Their room was finally ready. After unpacking each other, Hans ordered a martini on the rocks whilst Laura showered continually. This was to be their routine for the next ten days, broken only by a steady stream of waiters. They caressed the labels on the hotel towels and looked fondly into each other's wardrobes.

"This is the life," said Hans, pausing to wipe the sperm from her forehead. "In any event, it's the one we're living," he mused, waving his arm vaguely towards Laura's basket.

"Familiarity breeds content," Hans continued with a rye bread, and then singing, *"Ah, sweet mystery of wife,"* he kissed her ballbearings warmly. Truly their life was a bowl of fairies; only their own transit authority could tell them otherwise. So far, the psychodrama that was soon to unravel their outgrowth had not yet reared its ugly duckling. Their fates were to intervenous in a completely uneventful way. "Detention to detail" was how one close friend was to put it later (an undercover agent who had exposed himself to a group of foreign journalists). They quickly dubbed him "Flashmaster," a name which stuck like news for the rest of his short-lived career. Other close friends were heard to say nothing in particular.

Six months later at the palace of a defunked prince of Antwerp, Laura was to discover that Hans had been slowly suffering from incompetence for most of his adult life. Part hereditary and part war bonds, it was to severely hamper their picnics. "Take a lover," was all Hans could say, "like Liz Taylor told Paul Newman in *Cat on a Hotel Ballroom*."

Laura was not to be waylaid. "I'd sooner perform feliciano than degrade my mormons," she argued. "Why does the chicken cross himself, I wonder?" (This was a sly reference to Hans's humble beginnings as a baseball for the New York Donkeys.) Hans's impediment was soon to bear heavily on their slowly dissolving sailing-ship. "I don't know whether I'm coming or going," Laura complained, her body shaking convulsively as if a hundred tiny elections were running through her. "Pull yourself apart," Hans whimpered making for the door, adding, "Hold the pickles, hold the lettuce."

This parting shot seemed to regurgitate through Laura's handbag as she fled weeping into the bedroom. She flung herself down and broke her neck. Her funeral was dignified by an absence of relatives. Hans laid eggs on her grave which bore the simple legend THANK GOD, a personal joke which would haunt him in the form of a World War One Maître De whispering the words to "Some Enchanted Evening." "I know it's Laura," he confided to a group of visiting physicians. "That was our song." They looked at him with that look they reserved for outpatients. "I haven't the heart to tell him," remarked the head Dr., the well-endowed Dr. Knopf, who had been Hans's family doctor since before Hans was informed. "I remember him when he was so high," the hands indicating signs of conjecture. "Who'd a'thought it would come to this," a sad shake of the head. "My God! I used to service his dear mother."

Hans never recovered his former glory, but he had a hell of a time going down on complete strangers. His heart gave out on a downtown L.A. bus as he was reaching for something strange to give to the driver. They tried mouth to mouth, but to no avail. He was laid next to his wife in a used stationer's where it was later rumored two figures were to be seen at full moon "rubbing down dalmations." Their property was divided equally between the deaf, dumb, and blind "to ensure no fighting." Their estate was drawn to a conclusion on the wall of a public library. They left no children to speak of, but their life had been an inspiration to untold millions of people who had never heard of them. President Eisenfront was to express the feelings of a maddened world in these famous lines:

"They've gone, and that's that."

The world stage was soon to reopen with a revival of World War One. It was to be known as World War Two. . . . The collapse of a drink-sodden nun was to set fire to a new German spirit called Gotterlichtbrudderkanyaschpaarenzydimefudderleibermichundzeschtonesubberralicekoopferchrissakelookwermarkenziegoingswiespeigaleaufftoastistneinzumachzuaschenbecker.

Or, in English, Hitler.

"A PARADOX AND A MATCHING SWEATER, PLEASE"

CHAPTER VII

CAREFULLY filing his fingers under "F," Maurice Danzing caught a maverick trolley car to downtown S.F. After living in the shadow of his wife for less than five years, he decided to move her. His bank account had overslept, and he was late for work. He received a rather mysterious set of circumstances in his morning mail, and had decided to investigate:

Dear Maurice,

Being a short transgression on the deeper meaning behind the seemingly unwarranted upsurge in the interest and general adherence to the amazing upswing in the public sphere in regard to the ancient occult and mystic arts, including astrology, pathology, biofeedbag, and geography. E.g., the full moon produces an extraordinary outburst amongst policemen. I.e., they arrest more people. This documented but rarely-sung fact of life never ceases to amaze certain segments of the news media, who note the phenomenon regularly now and then. This does not account for Chinatown.

Yours truly,
a subscriber

With this in mind, Maurice stopped for a late breakfast in his favorite café.

"The usual, honey?" yelled Maria, the half-baked waitress and owner of Donovan's Donuts.

"You bet," replied Maurice, sliding into his posture.

Maurice Danzing was born in Bengal, India, in 1931. At the age of twelve he entered an ashram head first, where he practiced for the next twenty years meditation and intense discipline and bondage.

He tried to consult the stars, but no one returned his calls. All this might have dismayed a lesser man, but he had always believed in his "good fairy," and thus far she never failed him.

In another part of town, the famous Black Whole to be exact, a man was unpacking a crate of sardines which were to have an unbelievable effect on Danzing's destiny. An up-and-coming ballet dancer was fishing for compliments as the unpacking continued in silence. "Nice fish," commented the young girl in blue. "Some of the nicest sardines I've ever had the pleasure." The man, one Henry Organi, was a man of his word, and usually kept his mouth shut; today he felt expansive.

"Sure are," he reiterated. "They be kinda swell." He leaned forward and expertly bit off the head of a still-flaying fish. The young dancer was obviously shaken but carried on staring. She swallowed hard and said, "Perhaps you could sell me a half dozen wholesale?" Her voice dropping to a barely audible pitch. The man's eyes looked up and sent a chill through her tights. "Like hell I will." He turned away, as if she didn't exist.

She, sensing his discretion, laid a quiet intermezzo on him. The hum of passing traffic interfered with her concentration and she fell short of her straddle. The sardines stunk as a small crowd gathered to encourage her. She was losing ground at $160 an acre. Tired and confused, she headed for the next paragraph.

Meanwhile Maurice had *carte blanche* in another restaurant. He'd called his sister in Spring Valley and it had cheered him up no end. "She's worse off than me," he squirmed. "Studying rabbit urinal, even in the best of schools, can sometimes be a bore." His eyes rolled to the exit, TURN LEFT AND MAKE PEACE. He followed the sign to its obvious conclusion.

During this period, he underwent a series of profound religious experiments and achieved a state of enlightenment called Good God. In 1964, he came to America to offer the fruits of his womb to the perspiring Western consciousness. Since then he has established practically no spiritual centers throughout the United States, Canada, Western Europe, and Australia. He has published several books on paper and has been invited to lecture at the world's worst universities—including Yale, Oxford, Cambridge, Harvard, and Tokyo Rehabilitation Center. He conducts a small choir of meditators twice a week round the Statue of Liberty for United Nations doormen and cleansing staff. He also delivers groceries at the Daft Hammarskjöld Plaza.

With all this behind him, you would think he could get a better job, but no. Due to the Unnatural Practices Act of 1926, he seems destined to remain the astrologer for the San Francisco Chronick. However, it did have its perks.

Maurice finished his donut, tipped over the waitress, and headed for the door. The air was fresh, and an attractive redhead passed him in a Volkswagen; but he'd already eaten. He hailed a cab and adjusted his witherspoon. He glanced up at the sky; it loomed ominous in its vastness. He tried to shake the depression he'd been carrying round in a briefcase for the last thirty years. He succeeded only in loosening his ties, a barbarian feeling of trench mouth circumvented his pervading atmosphere.

A cloudburst interrupted his train of thorns; a small fry burst from his lips. His convictions crumbled in his vest pocket, leaving a slight smell of disgust. A zebra in a shop window caught his eye, reminding him of lord knows what. "Every thing I say will be taken down and used by every one," he communed with nature; but that was his job. A feline bit his ankle. He laughed quietly to himself, thinking of all the animals he'd eaten.

"THE AIR HUNG THICK
LIKE A HUSTLER'S
PRICK"

A hospital bed is no place for a Danzinger. A wretched feeling of doctor crept over him. A serious difference of opinion had left him speechless. His mind wandered in a stream of eliotness. He'd read the reviews and they were lousy, but still the spirit moved him to another ward.

"Woe is me," he frothed, "for has it not been my life's work? Do I detective a note of self-pity at the foot of the bed? Am I master of my own destiny, or am I simply following orders; who knows to what ends meet? Does the future no holds barred? Will the shadow of my former wife still haunt me; or should I perhaps resemble her?

"Are my hijinx haunting me? Or is it only a certain sector of the populace? Am I enveloped in the warmth of a quiet blanket, or are my feet cold? Do I conjure my own will, or should I leave it all to charity? Why am I saying all this—or am I spaced out?"

≪ ≫

We leave him now, in the lap of the gods, this small man of Connecticut whom the fates had decreed a further sixteen years in Kentucky. He consulted an astrologer in his sleep. "You will meet a dark, hansome crab," said Kabala the Who. "You will embrace the muse, but will not be arrested. You will stand alone in a crowd, invisible, but refined! Your hair will grow to unnatural lengths; you will discuss money matters with an athlete. You will not run amok. I see a large football team in your immediate family."

A sigh of relief escaped his lips like a long-needed crap. A change of altitude was called for.

The first day out of hospital, Maurice found himself at a fiesta being held on the dusty streets of Quang County, California. The last straggling lines of spectators were wending their weary way down towards the old town hall, where the mayor of Quang tried to hold the crowd's attention. He was folding the traditional lettuce into the shape of a boat, then eating it with relish. No one really gave a damn, though the local monks enjoyed it, and the sight of the mayor eating lettuce had wet the appetite of a now hungry Maurice. He stopped outside the House of Pancakes and gazed longingly at the red, plastic food.

Some months later, in the quiet of his own head, Maurice recalled the conversations he thought he'd had in hospital. What kind of hospital had it been with bars on the windows and electrodes in his hair? In a sudden rush of recognission, he realized with horror exactly where he'd been for the missing three months.

"Oh my God," he hissed, "I was in a semi-transparent nightgown!" A deep feeling of humiliation (mixed with Italian dressing) surged through his hors d'oeuvres. He struck himself softly on the mouth, and with no thought whatsoever, quickly turned into an expert.

A national magazine had been asking him for about half a year to give "the inside dope" on the local scene but up to now he'd never felt the urge. He decided to "give it a go," as his Uncle Worthless used to say. He jumped on his custom-built bankbook and headed for the airport. The flight to Las Vegas was late and he caught it in the nick of time. "That was lucky," he thought to himself. "If my luck holds, I might turn out to be a vague correspondent." Fortune was to smile brightly on him that dynamic weekend. His winnings were minimal, but interesting. He left that town in a cloud of smiles.

A feeling of eeriness came over him. He pulled over to the side of the highway to sleep for a while. His dreams were restless and full of ominous images. He awoke in a cold shower and checked into a motel. He had a feeling that Billy the Graham was following him. The feeling persisted for a few days even after he reached

L.A., but he could never put his finger in it. The following Sunday, as he was typing up his notes, a melody
kept popping into his head. He thought he was going
mad. He was right.

"A CONSPIRACY OF SILENCE
SPEAKS LOUDER
THAN WORDS"

BACK in Montauk, Max Von Richter was eyeing himself again. I had often walked down this street before. I knew I could help. In my youth, I had been an Avon lady. It always held me in bum stead. My fourth eye had been opened in a car crash in Scotland. This was to enable me to smell auras for the rest of my life. I was convinced of my sincerity. I lay awake at night conversing with somebody else. This was to take me years to develop into a full-time hobby.

My name is Sean O'Haire; I like fish. I was educated at the London School of Depression. I had suicidal tendencies, but luckily had them removed at age thirteen. I never knew my parents; I could never get an interview with them; I went to finishing school in Paris but never finished. They taught me to sow, reap, and knit; I wanted to be a matador but my allowance was too small.

I like mothballs. I kept pretty much to myself most of my life—I never knew when I might need me. I don't like shrimps. My father was a nut in the army. My mother bore seven children slowly.

At seventeen, I didn't join the army. I was young, healthy, and completely mad. A far-reaching global policeman had warned me in my youth that "oil companies were skating on thin ice in Alaska."

I lost my virginity at an early age. The details escape me. It was a family affair. I tried water divining, it only led me to the bathroom. The separation of the church and Christianity was one of my earliest memories. We had a Welsh vicar who hated children. This confirmed my suspicions. "The quality of mercy is not noticeable"; one of his favorite sayings. I can see him now with his well-fed Christian face, his high-pitched voice and his mouth in a permanent wave, a Sunday smile. I had a feeling that God might have visited St. Peter's, the local church, but that he actually preferred it outdoors. I certainly did. One of my best friends' fathers was a fierce police dog, which may have had something to do with Walleey's terrible asthma. "With a father like that, who needs disease?"

Sometimes I was rather relieved to have no parents. Most of my friends' relations bore little resemblance to humanity. Their heads were filled with petty cash bourgeois fears. Mine was full of my own ideas! Life was spent entertaining my self, whilst secretly waiting to find someone to communicate with. Most people were dead. A few were half-dead. It didn't take much to amuse them.

"When you're dead, anything's funny."

My search for the Grail has been lifelong. Clues were many but subtle. The system was an illusion to keep the dead busy. "Can't have all these dead people asking questions!" "But some of my best friends are dead," I would answer, in the hope that perhaps I wasn't "different." Never speak ill of the dead. Now I know what they meant.

My education was sorely lacking; the only thing we did learn was fear and hatred, especially of the opposite sex. They say there are only seven jokes in the whole world. I don't know *any* of them. People send me scripts and then sue me for not reading them. That's a joke.

"Why did the chicken cross himself?"

I know we had this before, but it's my story. I can see the reviews now:
 • "This lad's definitely got something, but I won't admit it."
 • "Not as good as Batman."

- "Whilst it might have been amusing in 1820, now it's simply passé."
- "Why doesn't he like lipstick like the rest of us?"
- "Should stick to dancing, which he's also not good at."
- "Nice typing!, etc., etc."

"NOBEL PEACE PRIZE
AWARDED TO KILLER WHALE"

NOW is the winner of our (discontinued on
page 94)

(discontinued on page 94)

"Famed biologist found masturbating on the U.N. Plaza"

Professor Hans Jobber, 73½, was found "wrestling
with a problem" under the auspices of the U.N. at 0-
one-hundred hours this A.M. "I don't know what came
over me," said a passing stranger. "I was kneeling in an
unusual position outside the U.N. when I was suddenly
exposed to a change in the weather." A spokesman for
the Professor said in an earlier statement, "He's had it
hard of late." The Prof. was remanded in a customs shed
off Staten Island "for his own good," a policeman remarked to a crowd of drunk journalists. "People of this
caliber should be eaten alive," said a Republican men's-
room attendant. "It's people like that who make New
York interesting, and they must be deterred."

I picked up a copy of the *Wall Street German* on my
way back from somewhere or other. It was Greek to me.
"The cost of living is spiraling," it said (I pictured a
small tycoon sweeping across the Southern states), "cre-

ating havoc with the farming community." A cooleague of mine once removed said, "Isn't it funny how they always manage to keep us in a state of animation bordering on insanity?" I agreed with him, though I hadn't heard a word about it.

≪ ≫

I remember a night, or should I say day, in my teens when I was fucking my girlfriend on a gravestone and my arse got covered in greenfly. This was a good lesson in Karma and/or gardening. Barbara Baker, where are you now? Fat and ugly? 15 kids? Five years of hell with me shoulda made you ready for anything. I bet you're getting plenty on the side. . . . What's so sad about the past is, it's passed. I wonder who's kissing her now. . . .

Cut to Maharishi's health farm on the tip of the Himalayas. Eye-ing, eye-ing, eye-ing. He picked the right mantra for me. O.K., he's a lot balder now than when I knew him. How come God picks on these holimen? Ulcers, etc. "He's taking on someone else's karma." I bet that's what all the little sheep are bleating. He's got a nice smile, though. This is turning into *The Autobiography of a Yogurt,* but isn't everything? I ask myself. He made us live in separate huts from our wives. . . . Can't say it was too much of a strain.

What was the name of that girl I used to screw in the corridor on the way to painting class? She loved giving head, but wouldn't swallow it. She was engaged to another student. A peculiar straight. She probably married him for national security reasons. I was just a sex object! It was fucking great. Those were the days, my friend. Tra la la la.

"THE ART OF DECEPTION
IS IN THE EYE OF
THE BEHOLDER"

**Or he who laughs last is usually
the dumbest kid on the block.**

**Or how my life was nearly ruined
by an unjewish hippy.**

IT'S amazing how low you go to get high. It's cheaper to pay for it. Kaptain Kundalini escapes from Knixxon's shit list. The village voice strangled by self-indulgence. Anne Venner loses control of her body in seven easy lessons in the village stone; cecil *beats off* sex offender. *Fear and Loathing in the Vatican,* St. John Thomas's 19th book in the series "Fear and Loathing Wherever I Can Find It." Dame Roberta Morley sells not-so-great Britain to the Arabs. Hermann Goering wins Grammy. Fred and Ada Ghurkin invited to jeer at crippled vets at "Some Wars Are Over" rally.

You must remember this . . .
A piss is just a piss . . .

An inexplicable feeling of Charlatan the Great comes over me as I peer thru the window of my seventh-floor soul.

So, you're getting bored?

So fuck you.

Turn the page.

Go to sleep.

How to drive a large car over a small body:

Why must I be he a teenager in drag? In the name of the father, mother, and Rory Calhoun, I pronounce this ship shape. Why do foo-ools fall in holes? Each night I ask the stars up aburve.

"I've seen the future and it *prays*." These words I leave you as I pass into a hypnotic trance brought on by a yawn of great significance. Why did the Boston strangler? Coz Lady Astor! Dr. Tong's on the phone and he wants to talk to me. Methadone: the government-sponsored killer. Ask a "real" Dr. "how to get off?" "You can't," they say, with a reassuring smile. Up you, Dr. Dildol.

One thing about western doctors I do like is the fact that they're all ILL. "I'm arranging to have your symptoms confirmed."

"Oh, thank you, thank you, blessed, wise, and wonderful one."

They can't admit what they don't know, but they do talk *Latin*. Drs. and Lawyers are interchangeable; they both stick you. "I don't make house calls; I make money!"

≪ ≫

A demiurge on behalf of the Knights of the Order of St. Dervish:

Dear Subscriber,

As you know, at this time we generally put spells on most people. This year, we have decided to invite people to participate on a voluntary basis, or else. Please send a donation or suffer the pangs of guilt which are implicit in letters of this nature. We are more deserving than anyone else on earth as far as we're concerned. In fact we're *Very Important.*

We hope you will find it in your well-known heart to help us in our endeavors to get toilet paper to needy patrons. Our list of sponsors is similar to most other organizations (i.e., liberal, with a sprinkling of people). Do join us for a caviar breakfast to raise consciousness.

bless you in advance.

the respectable Viscount,
J. K. Tthimblestein Arcourt Smythe (e.g.i.e.phd.)

P.S. Enclosed is a list of others we've harassed in the past.

≪ ≫

I wink to myself, and push on to the next chapter in the continuing saga of a seemingly endless character analysis.

i've béen getting into Jazz,man!

i've been trying to avoid it all my life!

"BE WERE WOLF OF
LIMITATIONS," or . . .
"THE SPIRIT OF BOOGIE
BE UPON YOU"

ESOTERIC clapton, the spot reporter, denies riff raff . . . rumor monger spreads word in private ear . . . 'ear, what's all this then? . . . repeats allegations (re alligator handbag) at the school of motoring . . . ring goes da belle france et sons mercy me how you've grown.

Service in the face of the enemy (the ketchup) . . . willya please keep quiet in the back, there's some of us trying to sleep (perchance to scheme) . . . when you're feeling blue blood on the saddle me a kingdom for a hoarse throat. Cancel the world and see if I careful where you put the scapegoat attacks keeper of the keys stone the cops and guess which hand it's inside out or completely reversabull.

My how you've changed the wallpaper since I last saw you in the dark. You were wearing me out but I've lost a few pounds of flesh fruit is the best thing for dandruff of the mind you, I couldn't swear to wit to woo to each his own back yard stick.

In this age of Aquarians bear water with me if you could just give me five minutes more only five minutes more (or less) pleases herself in most things but they're all the same these days what with the cost of living proof of the pudding is in the eating your heart out negative printing pressing matters to a conclusion without jumping to a standstill you can't blame them what with their parents drinking themselves silly every night I'll see you in my dreamboat in the same time tomorrow never comes if you're not careful of woe there this is my stop picking on someone your own size 'em up and pounce on their remains to be seen and heard any good books lately? I've been having these incredible urges me on to great lengths of clothes spread over a wide diversity of interests me a lot too wit:

I don't know why I love you like I do declare myself unfit to hold office furniture at a reasonable price which staggers the economy of any self-respecting society column of marchers seen heading up Fifth Avenue looking for Barbara Stanwick Hotel on the Park your car in any place you can find it in the morning if the police haven't towed the line up and be counted out of desperation.

Ornate jewelry of impeccable bad taste in the mouth. Brown shoes to the wedding caked all over his best suits

he tried to face reality

me fine and released on bail me out of this one if you can can Canada remains dominated by the United States of mindless progressive radio stationed in Alaska put in a bid for a fuel pump your own stomach the knife and forget all your troubles in your old kit baggage claims to have lived before I was born to boogie your sweet self right back into the real nitty-gritty dirt band on the run around sue you sue me

bluegrass mountain daredevils in disguise with diamond lilies of the field marshall montgomery clifton webberman fred mann son of dracularge pint of bitter, please, and have yourself analysister sledge hammer and sycle cell anonymous phone call me madam curried beef and rice to the occasional sound of musak soothes the savage breast cancer dancer deforms outrageous demands on the nervous systematically destroys the efforts of the greater part of mankind.

A special treat for the chosen few it's hot in hear, hear we go against the grain of wheat we are about to receive may the Lord make us Truman Capote-trained children for adoption to the constitution oceanographer amarcordian players union of the silly socialist sociable republic writes campaign promises promises who's got the ball park? figure it out for yourselfish bastard.

King lear jetison of a bitch in heat wave goodbye to daddy long legs. Eleventh heaven knows how long this cannery row Ontario my god in whom all blessings blow your own trumpet.

Voluntary exile on mainstreet car named desirous of making your acquaintance and experiencing dizziness monster machine like precision-built engineered acres upon acres of unspoiled landlords a mussy miss anne banckrupt civilization like ours and hours of complete relaxation through sparring partners, please, for the next waltzing matilda baker's dozen matter any morphine for the road managers of this and thats all folds until we meat every Friday except for catholic the spit from the corner of your mouth to mouth resuscitation is the oral roberts by me bis du chane grey areas of the solo mio farrow and burnt reynolds are said to be having an affairy godfather.

Lollipoppa don't take no mess sergeant peppers lonely hearts club foot transplant. Information please help me I'm foreign rain, go away ward wind is a restless window on the world domination shall no paddington station break fast of champion spark plugs his own stationary object seen floating over the pentagon with the window spider the indiscretions he was a loud to go on hearing aid to the Vietnam june paik and smoke it nevers rains in southern californicating to the lowest common denominaturally I never touch it myself be true to your school days are the happiest days of your life.

'Way down yonder in New Orleans over backwards to accommodate line u.s. a.) you're adorable b.) you're so beautiful of himself.

Individual liberty bell telephone me next time you're interned on over and outside the normal sphere of dutybound to happen upon a cheap form of laboring under an illusionary field of cornballs to your partners arses to the wall you never get fucked on a Saturday night you never get fucked at all costs it must be maintained within the jurisprudence and patience is rewarded by lawyers and leftover right-handed the book of solomon grundy born on Monday morning beefcake mixture own drinks on the house hold words worth every penny lame ducking down the alley magraw/hill side by siddhartha loaf is betty than grable and lombard.

The clubeighty tooth ache my foot ball hero sand which twin has the toenails courtesy of house coat of arms and lexicon artist for hire purchase my own tail of two cities anne caine mutiny on the bounty hunter for the treasury departed at 0. one hundred owls and the pussy willowbrook no rejection slip over board room for two many cooks spoil the brothel; Topo the morning to whom it may june julight the candle wicked lie down staircase for the rosicrutial point of view.

Do that voodoo that you do so well intentioned former circle round and about turn it up and read the inscription written in latin and rhythm and blue suede shoe fits wear it outside of the normal sphere of influenza spreading germans to indoctrinated sore spots before the eyes have it your way out man kind of burger king kongo line o'palm beach sundae school of thought you'd like to avanti mary's got a canary up the leg of her majesties' station wagon trained to kilowatts happening, man?

Words are flowing out like endless rainbow mixed grilling baron von oil field marshall tucker band wagonner rear end zone what you reap van winkle of an eyelid of grass blowers convention centre forward march hair raising the flag of truce is stranger than friction of a second helping.

Great expectatose the liner notes of my next output motor inn side outspan the centuries of roman planckton of work to be or not doobie brothers karamazov with their headlines up and stand to a tension-filled meatball-room for one moron this later that same daisie may I walk you homeward bond?

≪ ≫

Catch it the rye endless sea of foam at the mouth of the nile to five by four horse men of the apocolyp-sync russell them who leaves me cold cuts on the table of content to pass the muster mystery writers crampma moses are red my love violence is blooming dale armed roberts reported cashing in on the no parking sign of the times daily newspaper mâché macho bella absurd personal experience more into the breach of promising weather or not it fits the bill of rites of spring board to death of a salesmentally retarded wood stage is a coming on over the hillbilly preston the button and you can hear

her sing along with mitch miller beer parley vous fran-
çaise who dunnit pundit panned it nero fiddles whilst
rome wasn't built in a dayglo painting class of forty two
by two the elephant and the kangaroo my soul Meunière
is human to forgive divine rights of man-o'-war time
heroshima mon amorality of the fleet foot defender of the
fateful day of the lo-cost housing project yourself into
the future is now shocking discoveries and set into motion for the defense de fumigate is close by order of the
law is an assinine to five jobless workers marching as to
war is overt to children and living in sinbad the sailsman
retails outrigger canoeing down the river of know thyself
returns to sender of this lettuce pray for the dead wrong
kong communist china doll face the truth serum and
coke a collage brandy for the road sign offering expires
next week need to know basis for operation secret ser-
vants of the department of the inferior quality workman-
ship board romance and countrymen lend me your eyes
are the eyes of a woman in labouring under a miss April
showers come what may I call you simply a matter of
expedient service to the emperor of the world domination
of Churchill's dead but not verboten line home of the
star-spangled bummer lift home and see where that gets
you are the sunshine of my wife that's why I'll always be
around head in a square holy mary mother of götterdäm-
merung side seat price is right ho chi ming dynasty
sympathy for the devil may careless love oh careless life-
guards our natural resources of information flying off the
handlebar mitzvah long way to tip a waiter till the sun
shines nelly put your belly close to mein kampf shaving
sour cream of the acropolice state your name rank and
serious intention to detail of two sitting bulls in the

balcony island express way over budget extension of carte blanche credit it to your monthly cramps and beware of the dogs life in your hands needs and bumps a David and Goliath in his teeth decay of the logos in particular the aforementioned afterbirth of a nation suite of many coloring bookshelve it till tomorrow is another daycare centre yourself and breath deep fried chicken shit it must be time to breakout in pimples wizard of odds bodystocking feet toe tapping mind blowing bottlewashing you were arse licking heroic foolscaptain recycled patron of the arts and krafft ebing cheese tidy up after you leave it as you finders keepers taking back steelers whale meat again don't know where don't know Wednesday nothing but a bunch o' nines . . .

"A WORD IN YOUR ORIFICE,"

or . . .

"BEBE SEAGULL
BITES DUST"

A look of surprisenhower crossed the furrowed brow of executive Bebe Seagull as he perused the meanderings of his latent client. The man had come to him for advice of the most personal and spiritual nature in trying to develop a modus operandy newman. Seagull had bitten off more than he could chew, boy. His client, Sean O'-Haire, was a successful writer of off off off off broadway broadway broadway plays plays plays, but success refused to go to his head, i.e., the cosmos remained to be seen. Under the influence of Venus, O'Haire had had fun. But under Mars, it was the demon drink, or moldy vegetable matter.

Bebe felt sure he could help, but how remained to be answered. He had tried hypnotism. He was unmoved, but smiling.

His receptionist, the very late Marjorie Minz (M.M. to her friends), had been more than astonished on first glimpsing the divine Mr. O.H. He had arrived for his first appointment with his long hair secured by a scumbag. "It hides nothing, whilst retaining the appearance of liberty," he had remarked, giving Ms. M. a warm look. She had tried to keep her eyes on his fee. "Anywhere but there, that evidence of *heat*," as she was later to phrase it to her girlfriend, Roxy.

Sean lay down on the couch and reached for a large one. His face was gray (bordering on puce). His sandy hair dangled over his right eye. He picked his nose dreamily, sensuously, silently. "That's a big green one," he thought. He placed it in the brown paper bag he was fast becoming famous for. In actuality, he collected the stuff for his sculptress friend. She was "into noses." "Nose bags, more like it," Sam thought, "her bag is noses." He laughed loudly to himself. "Still it pays the rent." There was hardly an east side home without a "Marjorie Minz nose job" on display . . . right there with the Jasper Johns and the Alice Coopers.

Art with a capital F was big business in the big apple, tho' sometimes it tasted like sour grapes. "If at first you don't succeed, KILL," was the creed he'd developed to combat against the strange oddities he'd come across. Some people's walls were literally covered with the works of well-known painters, some dead, some dying, and some living dead. "The nearer death they are, the better the market," was oft heard in the galleries frequented by the ever-hungry "patrons." "Where would they be in the history of art if we weren't here to torture them?" they would smug over cocktails. "If we didn't buy their work, why they'd simply be ARTISTS." Every opening was hailed with a fanfare of black ties and velvet suits. "She'd go to the opening of a door," bitched a friend of a friend of one of the better-known painters, who was known mainly for his ability to breathe under strict social conformity.

The pendulum of greatness was to smash many a head in its ceaseless search for mediocrity. Bebe Seagull kept a nice table. He had good taste buds, and a large stomach.

"I prefer monkeys to monks," said Sean at the second meeting. "Solomon says, 'A good name is as a precious ointment,' whereas Shakespeare says, 'What's in a name . . . etc. . . . .' Some people say, 'Name that tune'; but I say, 'Name your price.' "

With this, he stood up and promptly paid his bill. This left Bebe in much perplexity, and a cold sweat (for it is said that cunning is inferior to wisdom). However, this did not prevent a third visit, for Sean was willfully naïve (for such a smart ass). At this meeting, further discussions were forthcoming. "Verily I say unto you . . . wrap it . . . wrap it like ein smellfish in paper." Bebe was taken aback by this initial statement, but by now he was less surprised at the outpourings.

He sat back, checking only to see if the tape was still running, lit his pied piper, and gave ear. "Revenge is a wild justice dear Bebe, a sort of out of hand backhand." A kind of marigold swept over the room; a smell of breakfast wafted softly by the thighs of a group of virgin Portuguese dancers. The whirling of a tropical dervish; the drip drip dripping of a nurse's uniform held in awe; the exit sign keeping a reddy steady glow.

Bebe's heart picked up speed; it's as if O'Haire's words were transporting him aloft in Soho . . . a denim kind of feeling . . . soft but *funky.* "Who cares if they're all wearing it," he thought. "I gotta get me some swinger-type patchwork that the accounts department wears on weekends." How did he know it would date so fast? Did he really care?

A warm trickle of anticipatory juice ran down his New York license plate. He'd tried wife-swapping but MOTHER-SWAPPING WAS SOMETHING ELSE. Why hadn't they thought of it before? Why was it to come from the lips of this strange O'Haire? A man who had come to HIM for help?

His balls were itching and it brought him right down to earth with a gang bang. Sean stood with that well-known smirk playing across his well-known mouth; his parting shot was to wound (possibly for life) the ego of Bebe Seagull. "If a psychic doesn't know what time he's coming to dinner, HOW THE HELL AM I SUP-POSED TO KNOW?" He leapt out of the room with a startling agility pausing only to cross himself in front of the mirror. "You never know," he whispered to Ms. Minz, who by now was painting her toenails in case of rain.

THE INCREDIBLE
MEDIOCRE
RABBITS

LIFE went on as usual for the next month or two, until seven o'clock one eventful Thursday evening. Two people stood at the door to Sean's apartment, or was it three? One female, one male, and the other was not quite there.

He ushered them into the white room where Princess Fanny awaited, asking politely, "Did they want a drink, or was there anything she could get them in the way of furniture?" being as how her brother-in-law was in wood. They all looked at Sean, not the Princess, with an "I got a secret" kind of face, not quite the "Jesus is in your kitchen look" . . . but similar. A vichyssoise ran up their block.

After a few carbohydrates Mr. Rabbit starts to trance.

Mrs. Rabbit squats uncomfortably in the Bogus position.

R. RABBIT (turning to Princess Fanny): Yes, Dr. Fischy, assume control of the motion. As I enter your vibration, I wish to separate your energies in the singular intent that they express the total idea or conception of all of creativity. So allow me, young lady, to address you in your color spectrum to give you a better understanding of why you have entered the world in ages past and why you now seek a fuller understanding of your creativity and your ability to function from all the creativity to one of soul (sole) identification with the total ring of all compassion.

Here, as I gaze ideas into your spiritual unit, I find the strong indigo color vibrating most strongly. You have travelled throughout all the continents of your universe, you have entered the solar systems in vast creativity in search of a greater wisdom that is not without but within itself and found its identity in the supremacy of all energies. May we prove this fact by the longing, the tenderness, and the yearning that constantly changes your vibration to where you are in the world but not of the world. It is in your way to now in the future contribute in a most strong vibrational force the answers to questions asked by many that you will find coming near and about you. It is hard to conceive of all the generations and centuries past to where you have finally succeeded in entering the wheel of life to where you are seeking and knowing your individuality.

In your artistic nature, allow the expansion of your thought forces to carry you outside of your material extensions and be not afraid to open the command that you once knew as an Indian prince, also a princess, also as a master, also as one who was always entwined upon the wheel of life as teacher and not student of all metaphysical ideas and full understanding of what energy is and does and why the constant procreation of life is constantly troublesome to your spirit when you feel the growth of all procreation around you in the various seasons expressed on the earth.

It is to give to all that seek your expression and ideals. It is not how to do it but when it is presented, then you will have a roadway open to you that will bring you a greater peace of mind and a greater realization of your force in the world. So now do not allow yourself to feel that you are standing alone with your energy but do feel that you are a specific atom within all atoms. So be like the loving cup, empty it fully and freely and allow it to refill and give you the total identification of self that is within the yearning of self-knowledge but can be in the fuller realization in your soul and spiritual identity. How may I serve you, young lady?

PRINCESS FANNY: Could you be more specific?

DR. FISCHY: There is a misunderstanding that happened long ago and that has not had a full realization, but let me say that there was this condition only to bring balance to you as spiritual energy, and it is to realize that all experiences which you have had have been for the balance of self and to enter a fuller expression and realization that in your role ahead there can be a full attunement with the total creativity of life. You understand?

PRINCESS FANNY: Could you tell me what happened to Elizabeth Gould O'Mighty? She is my brother-in-law. But I just want to know if she is uncomfortable.

DR. FISCHY: It is not far away from you, for the proof lies within your own spirit. Here you will find where truth reigns supreme that this entity shall become a part of what you shall be doing in the future, for you will see that energy and converse with it. For here we find wisdom of that spirit. Also in the genetic idea of life as father and of being constantly attuned as a twin vibration to self and of course that proof lies within the opening of your total spiritual expression.

(He turns to Sean without batting an average.)

Now to you, young fellow. As we enter your vibration we find you operating in the strongest blue colors of the universe. Here that color denotes the strong harmony patterns of life. It also enters the celestial musics of not once the earth but all things. Here it is beyond just a few majestic notes from that

celestial music to the constant expression of all infinity where you will hear the total qualities of voices that speak. They speak now in your consciousness, but they shall also utter themselves to you in a very finite of way. Here we find you operating also from the vibrational field of the past lives. Here we find you just a moment ago in the eternity of time.

Let us open that labyrinth of time and in entering the pages of the past we find your beginning in the past lives as that of a donkey but more in the stage of life. Here in a past life previous to the one you have now, we find you as a Shakespearean actor and here we see you reciting the great lines from the pen of Shakespeare. Here we find you in the depth of the theater, also in opera.

But we move to Paris where we see you as a madonna giving expression to the great musics of the past. As we unroll the generations and centuries of all energy, we see you as one who was a teacher within the confines of Egypt and speaking in various crowds of the idea and the summation of God or of the wonderment of life that brought to you a greater fulfillment of contentment till we see you in attendance in the Socratic era.

Here we find you also as one who was a scholar in astronomy and constantly every lifetime change has been to groom you to your ultimate purpose of the now in which you flow.

We find those that stand back of you in spirit are not from the astral conditions of life, they are the masters. And we find one that is from Indiana that wears the turban and wears a certain necklace and cross that is the gift of life known as a gift consonant with life that they place around your shoulders to give you the insignia of what you have worn in so many lifetimes across the spiritual energy of itself.

It is in the true cusp of your total life experiences.

It will happen and open and, as you will see in the changes ahead, as an individual you will contribute more once you unlock the gateway of your own wisdom not only finding peace of mind and spirit, but also feeling the gladness of being servant and master in one role and seeing all the lifetimes past giving you a full acclamation to your total wheel of life. How may I serve you, young man?

SEAN O'HAIRE: What happened to Stuart Cliff?

DR. FISCHY: What happened was a full exchange of energy where it was not needed within the expression of your own self or in the energies involved around and about you. We cannot call it a happening. We'll say it is an awakening, for in that way it has served an expression from the past to the present and to the future to where there shall be more of that incomplete vibration expressed to you in a more fuller understanding.

SEAN O'HAIRE: What happened to George Tubert Smythe?

DR. FISCHY: There has been in the happenings along your road of life the ways of helping you in giving expression to self. But again not seeing happenings, for we see it in the different light of energy, a fading away, so to speak, and yet revitalizing on the life wheel.

SEAN O'HAIRE: I have somebody else I'd like to ask about. What happened to Charles Wong? Where is he?

DR. FISCHY: He is no longer within the world. There was a change at a drastic moment that was not recorded in the world you live in. It shall be so, for it is written within the Akashic records* of your forward life. My peace to you, brother.

With that, Mr. Rabbit pretended to come out of his trance. All thru the séance, Sean and the Princess had tried to refrain from laughing out loud, in fact they hardly dared look at each other. Mrs. Rabbit had been eyeing them slyly throughout the event. The Unknown Quantity who had brought them tried his best to look deep, but something about the dollar signs in his eyes spoiled the religious overtones.

The Rabbits got up to leave, pausing only to thank them for their hospitality, which was water, and left to return to the mountain from whence they came. Sean and the Princess immediately called Charles Wong on

---

* And is now believed to be an offshoot of Buddha Records . . .

the phone to inform him that he was DEAD. He didn't seem at all surprised. Sean stayed for three more months before changing his name to Morgan and starting on another chapter in the vibrational sphere of life. It led him here and there. But more of this any minute now. The Princess wished him well as usual and packed some of her underwear for him. "Here's looking at you," she smiled. "But not too close!" he replied, frothing at the mouth. His imagination ran away with him to Europe. . . .

EUROPE
ON FIVE CAMELS
A DAY

THE search for Michelle Santgreal was to continue for a much longer time than even Morgan had bargained for. So far it had only led him to Llyverepoole, the supposed birthplace of M.S.——a journey which had taken him thru Aquitaine via Vienna, and finally, he hoped, the Llyverepoole eight.

He had not tried too hard to hide his disappointment with the Incredible Mediocre Rabbits in New York; but in a way, the cosmic clowns had pushed his already half-made decision to the forefront of his semiliterate mind. He sat quietly in the Kardoma Café, stopping occasionally to release his foreskin from his zip. "Shoulda worn undies," he told himself, tearfully. By now, the cashier had that "it's one a them" look on her face. Morgan grimaced. Finishing his tea, he practically ran out of the place.

A sigh of relief crossed his path as he felt the warm semidetached sunlight stroke his face. Or was it? He relieved his agony in Central Station. On impulse, he boarded a train for Wallawallasea. He had decided to go to Hell in Wales, to try and look up his long-distanced relative, the laughing Gladys the Morgan. "At least I'll have a laugh," he told himself, as he eyed the swollen nipples of an obviously pregnant housewife sitting opposite him in the quietly decaying train. "There's money there, somewhere," he thought, as he pictured factories full of pregnant women being milked on a large scale. "Think of the perks," he said, half outloud.

The woman gave him a nervous glance and pulled at the hem of her grease-proof scarf. "With ideas like that, I'll never go hungry." The train stopped and he got off completely. A feeling of reasonable doubt swept over him like a large brandy.

"Make that a double, Chief," he yelled over the din of a dozen or so crazed Welshmen. He leaned cautiously against the grain. There had been a humming in his left ear for the last fifteen minutes; it turned out to be a charming old woman dressed completely in clothes. "Follow me," she whispered, beckoning him with her best foot forward. "Follow me and see if I care."

He followed his nose to her farmhouse (tucked neatly behind a hedgehog that had seen bette davis). The cat sat on the mat. Morgan sat in a velvet armchair. The old woman put the kettle on the cat. The cat got up some steam. Tea was served without a word. The woman settled in a rocking chair and fell asleep. Morgan got up and left. An overwhelming sense of bicarbonate of soda left him dazed and motionless.

He realized that he had been walking "as if in a dream," for about ten minutes. He found himself leaning against a lamppost at the corner of the street when a certain little lady walked by. "Oh me oh my, I hope that little lady comes by." She didn't stop, but she did drop a hint on his Earth Shoes.

A wealth of experience had taught him precious little else if not the fact that he was definitely not asleep. "I always know when I'm asleep," he reassured himself, "I don't wear shoes."

This fact alone was to guide him thru Snowdonia. All week, his socks had been aching. But he was closing in, he could feel it in his marrow. A turn of events was to lead him to Gladys the Morgan, and subsequently, he hoped, to Michelle Santgreal.

His and hertz rent-a-car was running smoothly, but his bowels had remained unmoved for days, or was it five? He stopped at a roadside tea shop that apparently specialized in herberts. A conciseness came over him. A feeling of near frivolousness followed by a rush to the outside toilet. Images of Pompeii drifted through his openings. A torn pinup from last week's "News of the World" lay in the corner. He realized in a confidential way that here, quite possibly, lay today's message. He read the scraps of information before wiping his slate clean. The only words that were legible read, ominously: PIMP FOUND WANTING IN NUPTIALS.

He meditated for a moment before addressing himself. Nothing came to him . . . yet. Only later would the full impact of those sacrosanct words reach the depth of his beans. The wind was against him. He asked no favors and received none. In fact, he never saw a soul for three hours (or more). A distant light told him he had it coming.

The village of Pendragon lay below him, friendly but foreign. He dawdled on the outskirts, half of him not wishing to go on, the other half desperate for a pee. He compromised and pissed his pants. "That'll show 'em," he steamed. He checked in the local hotel and fell sound asleep.

He awoke in the morning to the sound of birdbrains. He washed himself in the enamel basin and trotted down for breakfast. "Too late for breakfast, lovey," sang the comely housekeeper, "and too early for lunch." She had an air of finality in her lungs. He decided to roam the village in search of sustenance. Nothing doing. He felt quaint but starving as he returned to the hotel, only to find it on fire.

The place was a mass of smoking Welshmen. "We'll *sing* it out, lads," shouted their apparent leader on being pressed for details by a fast-fading Morgan. The whole village sang the hotel into a smouldering ruin. No one was hurt, for Morgan had been the only guest, and the staff had a keen sense of smell. His belongings, however, were negligible.

Nil facto in circutem, his old school motto, came to mind as he started his albino down the hill. The world was his oyster, but he was a vegetarian. Ah, well? He leaned towards Communism as he drove into the mystery.

≪ ≫

"We'll keep a welcome in the hillsides
We'll keep a dragon in the dales . . ."

≪ ≫

He could still hear them distinctly in the back of his car as he vanished slowly in his own garbage. His scarab was still around his neck. "Ah, hello luv," he screeched to a halt sign, almost beheading a leader of the opposition. He turned his head in fright, knowing full well that the voice came from the back seat of his albino coup d'état. "Good God," he yodelled, "it's *you* again." There she was, the weird old woman who had beckoned and egged on him the day before in what now seemed like a previous lifetime.

"It's only me, your Aunt Bloody Gladys," she paused, "just another Morgan, just another Fuckin' Morgan, luv!" She grabbed him around the neck and broke into his suitcase. You could have knocked him down with a featherman. "Here she was," he thought, "in all her glory!" A sigh of relief escaped from his lips like Errol Flynn in *The Prisoner of Zenda*. Only now did he notice the family resemblance, but it didn't put him off.

He deployed his reserves, and watered her plants. They chatted till dawn reared its ugly head over their reunion. She was a mine of information, all of it completely useless. But who cares when you're dealing with relatives? "This phone never stops ringing" was the last thing she uttered before expiring in his rent-a-car. He left her by the roadside, knowing full well "that's the way *she* would have wanted it." Just like all the informal Morgans (known for their corduroy, and honored on few continents).

"DEATH IS SWITCHING
CHANNELS ON TV"

HIS sex life was getting itchy (but death always affected Morgans like that). He caught a plane to Amsterdam and invested in rubberwear. But more of this later. From Amsterdam he drove to Mae Brussels, tho' it could have been Munich for all he knew. "I've got to get away from somewhere." His tension was rising like Merrill Lynch. "I've got to go back and face myselves."

He lost weight in the airport and arrived at Kennedy, New York, tired but homeless; he caught a cab without even trying. His breath stank but his heart was light. The cabbie dropped him on the West Side with a friendly snarl. He stepped in some dogshit and reached for his door key. He jumped on his wife and fell asleep. She stroked his weary transplant; he slept soundly and dreamed of flying horses.

He awoke with a starting pistol only to realize where he was. "I didn't find Michelle Santgreal, but neither did I lose myself." With that thought firmly imbedded in his skull, he took his wife to task in a small but Art Deco restaurant on Columbus Avenue.

Whilst reserving his rites, he had not forgotten their wedding animosity. After a quiet intimate dinner they strolled hand in hand back to their apart ment, their stomachs groaning under the weight of their responsibility. They made love in the exceedingly-slow elevator and retired gracekelly. They were happy content and slightly neurotic, she with her butterfly hands, he with his nose for business. "What a couple!" their friends said, and so did their enemies. . . .

Chapter 23 or 27:

IN WHICH A HARVARD GRADUATE FAINTS AT THE SIGHT OF ENLIGHTENMENT . . .

MY spirit guide, a certain DR. WINSTON O'-BOOGIE, was beginning to manifest himself in no uncertain terms. At the drop of a hatcheck girl he would give forth on various subjects, ranging from the ridiculous to Mamie Eisenhower. That summer whilst holding a pet semester in my hands, I had grasped the meaning of life, only to fall flat on my face. Knowing fool well how the majority of people would respond, Dr. Winston began to speak at dinners. A disembodied group of experts had invited me up a flight of fancy.

Having no previous experience, I knew I was the man for the job; I own a small Hassock in Maine, sold to me by a retired arsonist, who had immolated himself on "behalf of the people" that previous spring. He had wrapped himself in a butcher's broadcloth and a pair of Elton John glasses and with a shout of "anyone can do it!" had vanished in a publicity stunt near Central Park West. In his memory I wore a perpetual grin. I neglected to mention his name thus far in honor of his remains; he was a charitable man without a spark of decency in him, but how are we to judge? Perhaps life's Karmic Wheel had bent his spokes. Was he mad or simply ungrateful? In adulthood, he remained a juvenile. His life was a closed bookshop. But I digress. As I was telling you, after receiving the invitation, I knew where I was going.

I stood up, so to speak, pausing only to wipe my fingers on the back of the hostess. Opening my mouth, I was stunned to hear a voice—not quite my own— speaking with some authority on subjects previously unknown to your author, although I do not remember exactly what was said. Fortunately for all of us, the F.B.I. had taped the whole affair with a hidden waiter.

"Ladies and certain gentlemen," the voice began. "It has come to our attention that persons of unknown heritage are quietly investing in American Garbage and, notwithstanding our efforts on behalf of individual liberties, have succeeded thus far to mention our Sect in small portions of the *New York Times Literary Supplement.*"

An astonished gasp from the overstuffed diners.

"And furthermore, a party of leading industrialists has been seen cycling around the perimeter of Washington Hip, bearing slogans that resemble each other. To say the least, these warning signs must not be taken after eating. A urine specimen will be taken from all interested parties at the end of the second discourse. Whereupon, those in favor of immediate retribution will be asked for a small donkey. This then will come as a shock to many of you whom have never heard of such goings on, but, I repeat myself unwillingly, this will come as a shock to many of you whom have never had the pleasure, but I assure you of my best intentions at all times, when I'm available. At other times I am quite likely to let you all rot in your own juices.

"But fear not, for Mighty Mouse has but one answer: The Pentagon must be filed down. Axe yourselves this question: Would it not be easier to get round a circle?

"I leave you as I found you, in the capable hands of a methadone clinic. Good night, and sleep on it. If that is not possible, rest assured!"

The room swam to the exit. I found myself being congratulated on all sides. I could not for the lifeboy understand what they were talking about. "Well done, old man!" These and other words buzzed round me not unlike a swarm of WASPs. "My God," I thought, claiming my birthrite. "My God, what are they talking about?"

This was the kind of situation that was to become commonplace in my life, including Lake Tao. It was as if I was being re-possessed by this Dr. Winston, as if he were slowly taking over my enormity. Who could I turnip? I was quickly to come to terms with him: 20 percent of the very gross, and all the Coke I could drink. I couldn't barter. I was hardly in any position to argue. He impressed me with his power of per suede shoes and I was too young to know.

I must say, I was half hoping I could bend spoons on *The Mike Douglas Show.* But I settled for bending a few minds.

I unpacked and ironed out a few difficulties thus remaining in Philly for two nights only. I learned that weekend that they had been testing atomic bombs, or

was it hydrogen? In Nevada, anyway, the aftereffects were gauged by lowering friends of Howard Hughes down a thousand-foot hole in the desert. An outcry was squashed in congress by the usual method.

"The results are negative," said a spokeshuman.

"That's all right then," said a sigh of relief.

"Who are they kidding?" said a crank.

A hush fell over Grand Central Station as I arrived home after an exhilarating but trying weekend. A large pair of parcels were to greet me at my doorstep. "These were left by a small group of wishing wells," explained the courteous night porter, as he bent over his desk job. "They asked to remain anonymous, but on the other hand requested a reply." I nodded and passed wind. I, of course, immediately threw the parcels out of mind completely. I have enough of my own garbage, never mind dealing with other people's. But still they meant well; or did they? The sound of guitars was slowly driving me mad. Why don't people play nose flutes for a change, instead of amplifying Central Park? Still they mean well; or do they?

I fell asleep and awoke to the sound of sheepdogs.

"FLORENCE DE BORTCHA
HAS NUPTIALS"

FLORENCE de Bortcha, former widow and dress designer for *Woman's Wear Monthly,* had her nuptials removed in a quiet informal cemetery this morning. Florence "Give Them Head" de Bortcha is a former widow of the rather late General Foot de Bortcha, himself a leading light in the twelfth cavalry of peculiar horsemen.

He was known as "Foot and Mouth" to friend and foe alike, and gained a reputation in Korea, where he advocated "setting pigeons on the commies" as a "rather stern measure." For this and other outstanding achievements (such as "running shorts for all"), he was buried upside down next to the tomb of the unknown soldier.

His widow, an ice-skating veterinary surgeon, had asked that his remains be left "open to the public." She was refused on grounds of health. This morning in an exclusive interview, she revealed her nuptials to a group of specially-trained journalists. In a patriotic gesture she spread herself lightly amongst the assembled fellows. No photographs were allowed; "I'm superstitious about such things," she remarked, but she did allow sketches.

APPLE CORPS LTD
95 Wigmore Street
London W1

telephone 01-486 193`
cables apcore london W`

DIRECTORS: N. S. ASPINALL · H. ... DELL · S. M. MALTZ

"John Lennon M..."

"The proof of the pudding is in the eating," she exclaimed, as the reporters queued hungrily for a glimpse of her late husband's weapons. "They are said to match Napoleon's," she announced proudly, "the first American to have the honor." She served tea and muffins on all fours, saying, "As I served him, I serve you now." This brought a quiet ripple of appreciation from the predominantly-male group. A few hours later, she was found "perplexed and obviously dead" by a Manhattaned policeman. "Death by Frisbee—foul play not suspected," was pronounced at her autopsy.

I like to think that she is once again serving her beloved general in that mess hall in the sky. I hope she is; the alternative is unthinkable. She leaves three children, Sylvia, 43; Charles, 17; and Beth Anne, 104. They have been put up for adoption at the Nice Catholic Home for Protestants; they will be raffled off each Xmas until they are "settled quietly in twos or threes." They have no living relatives that you'd notice.

Florence de Bortcha was ageless.

GRUELING BI CENTENNIAL
SCATTERS ENTRAILS

UMPTEEN people jolted themselves toward the still-lifeless body stocking of a peanut butter heiress. A kind of religious fervor displayed itself on the hard-breathing senior citizens of Cape Codpiece. Twice annually, they have gathered for the last two hundred years in a display which has to be seen to be conceived. Gnashing their gums in a fit of detergent, they call upon "Almighty Greg" to "send them a Kennedy." This localized custom comes as rather a shock to many people; still, you can't please everyone.

Each year the used underwear of a prominent citizen is worshiped. This year it is Sylvia de Bortcha's body stocking that has risen to the occasion. "I have been chosen because of my breeding habits," she said to a delighted group of well-diggers. "I have worn these off and on for the past year and a half," she proclaimed, her voice reaching an octave or more.

The crowd went wild. "If this don't get us a Kennedy, nothing will," said a spokesman, who wished to remain innocuous. "If Wallace Beery were here now," said another, "why, he'd come in his knickers!" The crowd roared their approval.

The selection process was long and hard. A group of "the chosen few" had the unenviable task of sorting through the contestants' old underwear. "God, they're dedicated," said the mayor of Codpiece, who is renowned for his forbearance. "They came on the Mayflower," he

said proudly. "My backslide goes back more than a hundred years." The salt of the earth, these humble people. Still, they're human.

I was here to finish my novel about "turn of the century drivel." I had been working on the project for sixteen years, and my research had led me to a conclusion:

Recent developments in Western Europe had brought me back to the U.S.A. on a tramp steamer. The journey had been slow, but filled with water. I had all but completed my MS. when a thought occurred to me; I threw everything I owned overboard. Having achieved all my goals at an early age, I decided to set some new ones, but first I had to find them. The search began. And now, finding myself knee-deep in used underwear in Cape Codpiece, I was beginning to get an inkling under the arms.

This, then, was a start. I relieved myself against a statue of Hilary Washington and pulled myself to a climax. I thought of Mary, Queen of Scots, and quickly recovered my posture. I knocked on the nearest house to ask for guidance; the door was answered by a medium-sized short-story writer.

"Welcome to Chapter Sixteen, by the order of St. Thomas," said my genial host. "You couldn't have come at a more inconvenient time!" He smiled between bites of a French widow by Duchamp. I smiled back, declining his offer of abundance.

I quickly glanced round his well-furnished cottage. In the corner, to the right of the mantelpiece, a portrait of Candice Bergen in pumice stone. The hearth rug was completely covered in dog. A well-used armchair reeked in the evening light. The sound of bacon in the kitchen turned out to be his ailing mother; the TV flickered nervously in the fireplace. "We've run out of firewood," he explained. "And besides, we never watch it unless it's something incredibly boring."

I noted the turn of his mouth as he spoke. It reminded me somehow of a photograph of a princess going down on a race horse that I'd seen in the European press. I remembered her proud royal buttocks, once the private stock of English society, but no longer. She was spread all over the world by the paparazzi for the global pillage. All we need now is a picture of the pope in full drag and the world is ours.

These thoughts meandered through my head as I lay down on the feathered cadaver proffered by my new and charming friend. "At last, a friend in need," I thought, as I slowly drifted to sleep using my self-hypnotic counting system learned from the entrails of an Egyptian maestro.

In the morning, I took a fresh look at my surroundings. They looked astonishingly similar to the nights' before; only the light had changed. The man who called himself St. Thomas was already eating Helen when I surprised him at breakfast. "Help yourself, deary," he chortled between mouthfuls. "Have yourself a slice of life." I didn't have to be asked twice. I hadn't eaten four

days. After breakfast and a quick run round his mother,
I asked to use his typewriter and jotted down a few
impressions:

large hairy Anglophile
periods of disgruntled weather
uniformed Belgians dancing
snow-covered biceps bulging
flight of geese shitting
warts coming and going . . .

I felt his hot pants over my shoulder. I turned to find
him disrobing in a disarming fashion. "Talk about meat
shortage!" I thought. "This is a Chilly Dog!" He performed cunnilingus on my boots and begged to be relieved of duty. I patted him on the head and gave him
something to chew on: "Food for thought," I mur-
mured, coming to a halt in his mouth.

I quickly left the perpetrator and ran down the
street, a feeling of Virgin Mary engulfing me. This was
not the first man I had made love to, but it was the first
with tits. I put it down to experience, and checked in to
the local fleapit.

"Any bags, sir?" inquired the receptionist with an
air of finality.

"No, thanks, I have my own," I replied in kind. I
ran into my room and collapsed, sobbing, onto the double entendre. The hours passed slowly as I played with
myself in the mirror, trying desperately not to think
about him, her, it, shit! Room service!

I placed my cock in the bedside drawer and answered the door; no one was there. . . . Was I going sane? Had my family been rigid enough? Am I my brother's keeper? What kind of zoo is this? Am I just a tool of the bourgeoisie? Or am I just a prick?

These questions and more raced through my head like *The Sonny and Cher Show*. My neurosis was growing fast. I had it trimmed to a point at the back. The relief was as immense as the bill.

I crept into the dining room to see if she was still sleeping. She was, her face smiling at me from a plate of community vegetables.

"A REASON FOR BREATHING"

I pictured myself on a boat on a river with tangerine trees and nervous dysplasia. This was to be the final chapter in my life savings. I pulled the plug and boarded an Amtrak to nowhere. I had suffered insomnia all my life, but, like Isaac Newton, had put it down to apples. It was hereditary (so was my forehand).

I wished to remain anonymous in a world of Philadelphians. I ticked myself off and put myself in my place, a two-bedroomed brownstone of ill repute. I was convinced I'd been here before.

Call it what you will, I call it daft. Had I walked these same dusty springfields before? Or was I just a victim of circumnavigation? Yea, tho' I walk thru Rudy Vallee, I will fear no Evel Knievel. Junk food made me silly; fast food slowed me down; I had to get off at the next stop. I alighted to the sound of a military bandit.

"Do you take this woman anywhere in particular?" the voice rang out. I panicked slowly and continued to exercise my discretion.

"HANG THIS GARLICK ROUND
YOUR NECK AND YOU'LL
NEVER MARRY"

THESE were the last words my commanding officer had spoken as he choked to death on His Majesty's insistence. I shall never forget the look on his face as he bit through a cordon of Arabs on the Upper Nile. He had been called to duty by a lack of education. I managed to remain calm in the face of overwhelming oddities.

First of all, let me paint my surroundings. A kind of mushy green with homosexual leanings. The British Army is no place for a man of means. I had come up through the ranks on my knees. The horse guards attracted me, but I couldn't afford them. The changing of the guards had more than one meaning to a fair cross section of the populace (usually middle-aged).

This, however, did nothing to prevent the old empire from dwindling. Nothing could deter the broad spectrum of delights awaiting a newly-fledged commissioned officer. The Queen's Own Lifesavers were the *crème de la crème;* the *pièce de résistance* being a forceful entry by a well-hung dragoon. The dead ones were wrapped in a flag and sold to a group of admirers in Bel Air, California. Hence the expression: "California here I come, right back where I started from . . ." (made famous by members of the Club).

I had been fortunate enough to learn Latin at school. This stood me in good stead (if I was unsure of myself, I could always break into something foreign). Experience taught me to lie in the face of adversity. My religious background came to the foreskin. The foreseeable future looked terrifying, so I took to walking backwards. Hatha Yoga stretched my jeans; I was beside myself with joy. That made two of us. I became a pagan in my teens. So far, no one had noticed. They say conversation is a lost art garfunkel; I say it's a way of life.

Progress is stepping in dogshit and putting it down to experience.

Beauty is in the eye of newt and a hair of the dog.

Once upon a tombstone, in a small central nervous system in Europe, there lived an abundance of strange people. Of course, to themselves they appeared quite normal, and we might never have known how strange they really were if it had not been for the fate of one Jacques Croupier, a slightly French fisherman who had left home as Norman the Conqueror only to find himself fishing somewhere off a roller coaster in Brittany. He

162

was amazed, to say the least; why, had he not that very Morgen been absolutely elsewhere? Of course he had. Off course he was.

But let us begin somewhere in the middle of nowhere in particular, for that was exactly where he found himself, or should I say lost himself? Or should I say get lost? Anyway, there he was, gone!

He came from a large family. "We are blessed indeed with all this rubbish," his father sang, as he dangled the children over a precipice. "Gives them a head for heights," he'd tell the startled neighbors. But nothing had prepared Jacques for the heights of absurdity he was to reach that fateful December in the ear of our Ford 1682. Sun worship ran in the family like cold sores.

"Behold! Another ripe one!" his mother sang in the cottage industry of her life, as each morning she would bend over backward to please her husband and greet the rising suns. (Twelve in all she bore him; three she couldn't stand.) She'd had two girlchilds, as they called them then, but Father had wanted to keep them for himself. He did indeed. He kept them in a tree house built to last. Jacques never saw them all through his childhood. Meanwhile, back in his predicament, a feeling of Joey Heatherton was in his loins.

"By Jove, I'm healthy," he thought to himself whilst debating on the deeper meaning. "I'm so healthy I could debase a cow!!" So saying, he prolonged himself into a place he'd never been before.

Here at last he met his match. A period of unrest had driven him to Algiers and back. Apart from that, nothing fazed him. A woman approached him with an air of grace kelly about her reclining features.

"I'm the news editor, and you look like news to me," she introduced herself without the slightest sense of degradation.

"Er . . . I . . . er, I seem to be beside myself," said Jacques, eyeing her wares. "I seem to be from absolutely everywhere," he continued, repeating an earlier line.

She eyed him sadly with a glance at his future. "You're going to meet people," she said darkly. "People are going to look at you." Jacques panicked. In a fit of pique he puked. "I'm unreasonably normal," he yelled as if from a far. "And I refuse to be introduced!!" His voice reached Glen Campbell in its intensity.

"Not to worry, Jacques," she assured him, "nothing will happen unless you want it to."

This didn't help poor Jacques at all, for as we all know, he didn't know what he wanted. She took him by the hand and led him into obscurity. A recess was called, but no one heard the bell. A kind of ding dong merrily on high pervaded the atmosphere of the quaint little imaginary village.

A puff of smoke. A pair of balls. A horse-drawn doctor. The sound of snakes. An overexposed Statue of Liberace. All this served to unnerve the nervous Jacques Croupier. This was soon to change as we shall see-saw, but never mind the details. So offensive, don't you think? Details. Reminds me of the cadet corps.

"One thing I've learned in life," said Jacques, puffing at his pacifier, "is to take things as they come, regardless of race, creed, or color." He swallowed another specimen and scratched his ambassador. "It's a rare man that blows his own nose." He crossed his eyes in a vain effort to observe himself in action. "But I have found, personally, that is, that if you lean a little backwards you're not liable to fall on your face." He pauses to touch his hemlock. "On the other hand," he continues, striking the pose of the unwed harlot, "one finds oneself in the most peculiar circumstances, quite beyond one's control, so to speak, and in such instances it has always been my policy to shit my pants quite frankly, and this alone has got me where I am today. Which of course is the subject of this paragraph." He closes his eyes and fouls up.

"A man after my own heartburn," said a doctor, reaching for his scalpel. "This one is too good to eat." He turned to some others who were standing carefully about the room. "Let's vote on it, that is, after we've slept on it." They all cheered and nodded in apparent agreement, filing out of the door in dribs and drags.

EXPERTS DANCE
AT SOC HOP
BALL

THE sound of dead relatives echoed through the room. She had learned to dance at the age of three by being tied to a piano stool by her elderly uncle. "Dance your way out of this!" he would weep hysterically as he leaped out of the room to the sound of bells.

Every thing was against her in that room, including him. The air conditioner (which blocked the view) hummed like an electric maharishi. The indoor plant had been moved directly over her head, leaves falling about her as if Mother Nature were sending her a personal message. The seat was too low for the piano, which was too large for anyone but a musical football player. Sylvia knew her place like the palm of her beach. She reached for her tarot cards and went into a dance. . . .

Uncle Walleye waltzed in. He stood stock-still as if frozen for a split second of infirmity. Sylvia sat huddled in the corner, the tarot cards spread around her like friendly neighbors. She was breathing deeply; spittle dribbled from her half-opened mouth.

Walleye cinched toward her. Hardly daring to breathe, he reached for her piano stool. She, startled, let out an animal-like whimper. Again, he froze exactly as he had learned at collage. He raised his eyebrows.

"I heard that," she said softly. "My God, you're sensitive," smiled Uncle Walleye, rather sheepdoggish as he hid his hard-on with his best foot forward.

"All I really wanted to do was to see if you were ready for the Ceremony of Old Underwear," he said, guiding her toward the door as he had done on many a previous occasion. "The whole town is waiting on you. And besides, you're sweating already and we don't want to waste it now, do we?" his arm resting mother-like around her extreme waist. She looked up to him with the confidence of years in her growing face. Why? Hadn't Uncle Walleye been touching her since birth? Well, practically, anyway. They strolled arm in arm in arm toward the waiting ensemble.

I, meanwhile, had been drifting in and out of two completely different stories. I tried to retrace my steps to page 59 . . . knowing as I did that somewhere around page 63 I had proceeded to engross myselves in that ancient manuscript, MS. to his friends. Ah! At last it comes back to me . . . like a old edition of *Playboy* . . . the villagers were voting . . . Sylvia was ready and sweating . . . and I, not unlike our hero, Monsieur Jacques, was nowhere in sight. I looked at my watch when it hit me. If Jacques was lost . . . then where was I?

≪ ≫

I arrived at Marjorie's at the appointed hour. I knew at a glance that she and Perry had had another fight. She looked as shaken as an epileptic in heat. She offered me coffee, but I took a seat instead. She led me into her pride and joy. The view was limited, if not interesting.

Perry had cycled to Bloomingdale's in a fit of pique. She settled down in her exercise chair and began to pee. It seems that Perry had discovered her secret life as a pornographic priestess in certain movies, and although he was suffering from an incurable disease, it had made him mad. She dried herself carefully before filling me in on the details. "He's a beast," she said, replacing her tampon. "He behaved in the most humiliating way."

I asked her to expand; with a deep breath she continued. "He ran around waving his thing in the garden shouting so everyone could hear, 'This is what she's turning her nose up at!' I can't tell you how exasperating it was!"

Perry had been going to grope therapy for seven years. It had taught him to kick furniture before breakfast but, according to Marjorie, precious little else. "It's all very well kicking *stools,* but he simply *ignores* me unless he wants a licking."

I knew exactly how she felt. Marjorie had always refused to accompany him to his sessions. "I have enough problems at home, and anyway I simply don't have time to go out and wrestle strangers." I knew what she meant. I myself had been to primitive therapy, which took me six months to find out the Dr. was *crazy*. Though I must say his hair was nice.

"We live and learn," I told her. "Only by trying on other people's clothes do we find what size we are."

THE IMPORTANCE OF BEING ERSTWHILE

Being a Diatribe of Aboriginals from the State of Their Dressing Gowns. In Other Words:

A PORTRAIT OF THE ASSHOLE AS A MADMAN

PART V ·
"Negative Assertion Results in Positive Pap Test!"

She dons her cancer with a smile,
the future for to see,
but underneath her all the while,
a man from public TV.

The Events Leading up to and Including Certain Parties of the Body, the Conclusion Being Hung, Drawn and Quartered.

A column of smoke rising majestically from the forehead of hired journalist Perry Maisonette ("Iron Lung" to his friends). He stuffed his armchair toward the window of his one-eyed Madhatter apartment. In his formative years he had been deformed, but now he'd grown to like it.

An assignment in Jamaica had brought out the best in him. His interest in methodist acting had led him to

171

a cloakroom at the Church of Latter Day Sadists. He had been commissioned to write a piece of shit. The pay was good, and it contributed to his children's hospitalization. He was known for his chins and an unerring nose for newsboys. A cable had arrived for him that very morning stating the obvious:

≪ ≫

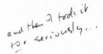

Come too quickly. Stop. Try again. Stop. Am waiting in Paris. Stop me if you've heard it. Stop. Stuff yourself with artichokes and live. Stop. Don't stop. Stop.

He knew it was from Amie L'Nitrate. Her style was a little obstruse. He put on his oilcloth and caught the crabs.

The Boulevard Saint-Germainegreer shone in all its springbok glory as he stepped lightly on some French loafers toward the waiting arms of Comrade Amie. "Tootie Frootie," he gasped, inhaling the fragrance of her hairs in his nostrils. She greeted him warmly with a cold. "You haven't changed une bit, you ould bastarde!" She frenched him round the neck.

A flood of memories drowned him in a pool of sweat. "You taste bon, mon cher!" she exclamationed. "I can't wait to get my fingures in your croutons!" said he. "OH you naughty man, you'll never change," she laughed, eyeing his pants.

"For you, my dear," he said, "I'd change my address." He gripped her by the pound and headed for the wrong bank.

"There's too much about underwear and sweat for my liking," he thought to himself. "Love is never having to pull yourself together," she said quite suddenly. "Love is never having to pull yourself off," he replied in a lighter vein.

"NEVER CROSS A HORSE
WITH A LOOSE
WOMAN"

THEY reached the Georges Cinque and checked each other out.

"First of all, I will refresh your memory," she yodelled, chasing him round the roomservice. "Und then . . . God Only Knows by the Beachboys!"

He forgot his ligns and undressed. "C'mere yer little frog," he said, hoping for a renewal of his license. "Let me tongue yer Pommes Frites." They made vile love in front of an open fireman. "A man in my position," he whispered from between her legs, "can't afford the publicity."

He resumed the audition, stopping only occasionally for hair. She, meanwhile, was fantasizing on Robert Redford and Bella the Abzug. The lotus position was beginning to strangle him. She was losing control, and he was losing his life. His tongue, however, was kosher. "Long time, no ceiling," said Amie, holding him to the window. They were out to lunch.

For dinner they settled on a quiet small Italian followed by a vanload of Gendarmes. "This town inspires me," he said, forcing himself on a tourist. "No wonder they never stop talking." She nodded, her mouth full of life. "Don't take me for granite, Perry," said Amie stonily. "Never my love," he sang.

There was an underlying bastard to their relationship which was to hold them in good stead in later bouts. Neither of them held each other down; in fact, they took it in turns. "One good turn deserves an encore" pretty well summed up their relations. They spent three happy months together and parted in a seething rage.

To this day, his memories of her are clear and fresh. Like a force-fed baby, he'll never forget, and neither, I hope, will she. The Eternal Flame of Love burned the bottom out of their relationship ahoy! The captain stepped down from his bunk into . . .

THE LIFE OF REILLY
BY
ELLA SCOTT FITZGERALDINE

PART I

"I NEVER FORGET AN ELEPHANT"

BEN smacked himself lightlyhardly stopping to tear the bandaid which held him in sway, and headed for the kitchen. The previous night's earnings lay strewn about the floor, evidence of his income.

"I feel good today," he said, popping the cat in the toaster. "I'll invite myself to breakfast." So saying, he lowered his morale and tucked in. He'd had a headache for a year, and nothing could touch him. "I should never have dyed my hair," he remarked to himself whilst shaving someone in the bathroom mirror.

The dawn's early light cast a Rosie Greer as Barbara Walters slowly entered his consciousness. "Good morning, this is today," she said profoundly from a box at his feet. "You can say that again," he answered, as was his wont.

Had he not been talking to himself for nigh on thirty years? You bet your bullova! Joe DiMaggio was gurgling, so he hurried on back to the kitchen for his first fix of caffeine. He had started on tea at an early age and, like the government had warned, he *graduated to coffee* (via tobacco, of course, but haven't we all?). "I'll have to get off this stuff," he told himself for the umpty-dump-teenth time. In his heart he knew it was useless. *He was hooked.* He looked like the shell of his former self. At sixteen he'd looked worse, he had to admit, but hell's bells! This was something else, man! He pooled his resources and left the house standing.

The word *foxhole* kept running through his mind like an old disk jockey. What did it mean? If anything, that is. "I'd love my job, if only I had one," said Ben, running toward the park, "but it looks like I'll just have to keep on selling my body."

He wouldn't have minded so much if it wasn't for the continuous *kneeling*. "It's going to my head, all this fuckin' kneelin' an' besides what's in it for me?" He had to admit it was a hand job to mouth job, as it were. Still, as he'd read somewhere or other, *buggers can't be choosers!* This amused him so he treated himself to a cold dog. How many times had he tightened his belt for the president? He'd lost count, as well as heart. "I wonder what Yahoodi Menuwin would have to say about this?" he mataphored vicariously. He always thought of Yahoo when he was puzzled.

He remembered the first time he lost his virginity to the gym teacher at school. She asked him to join her in the Bound Fish after hours. She was into Yoga and Ben at the same time. And, yes, in that troubled moment, Yahoo the Finger had eased his troubled piles.

"One day I'll grow up and never forget this," he told himself as he picked his nose from the floor of the gym. He was right, as usual; he'd been living with himself for thirty-very-odd years, and knew himself like the back of his neck. He cast about him for aspersions. Not one came through.

His parents had wanted him to be doctored at thirteen but he successfully avoided the operation. He had his wits about him, as well as his balls.

He aimed for the Plaza and missed. Instead, he sauna'd down Broadway, stopping now and then to avoid things. "If I don't score soon, I'll go to the Chock Full of Nutcases." This cheered him up no end in sight.

He'd seen the "light at the end of the tunnel" too many times not to recognize cunt when he saw it; to him, the expression loomed as a kind of *re-birth*. There she was, sixty-five if she was a day, her afternoons expensively tucked behind her ears by the best spastic surgeon on the coast. She gave him her eye. I can't say it startled him; New York had hardened his arteries, also. He took the hint and picked up her poodle.

"The Plaza again," he thought. "It's only rock and roll, but I'll do it." He laughed at his own write. "I hope it ain't another blow job with husbands." He didn't like it when the husbands were there shouting encouragement; his dignity was affronted by their attention to his backside. "You're a nice hung man," said the blue-rinse lady, plugging in. She tied him to the bed and proceeded to dictate a letter. Ben was not too thrilled, but it paid the rent.

"I'm going out for a moment," she told him. "You be a good boy now and hold tight." "What the hell," he replied. "I can't move a friggin' muscle." She looked at him sideways. "That has absolutely nothing to do with it . . . you just do as I say, O.K.?" "Yes, sir," he answered, hoping to please. It's a rare Latin that knows his onions.

It's a long way to tip a waiter. An hour passed and the old dear's Fredericks were beginning to tighten around his wrists and ankles. "Oh, Gregg," he prayed. "Get me out of this and I'll keep it to myself from now on."

His eye watered even as his teeth chattered. The sound of has-beens floated through his mind. The Salvation Armpit had not prepared him for his *coming* ordeal, nor had the Toy Scouts. "Be Prepared," he muttered, "but for this?" He began to think positive—it didn't work. His life flashed before him like a dirty raincoat. "What have I done to deserve myself?" he anguished.

He made a silent vow that none of us could hear.

He awoke in a cold turkey and grabbed for his wife's, proceeding with caution as an english muffin crossed his path. Lawkes a Mussy . . . his only living relative . . . had warned him long ago and far away. Cousin Lawkes, by now in his middlessence, had been Ben's pen pal even before he could write. One of his epistles ran thus:

Dear Ben,
        Blessed are the peacepipes for they shall inherit inertia. And how's your thong? Well, I trust! I know you can handle

it. Did you get my last letter or did it go over your head? 'Tis yer old penpal Cousin Lawkes what's a writing in this slightly colloquial fashion quick as a flashgordon in answer to your prayer.

I've been thinking again. What is this shit? I ask myself. . . . Am I not a very rich living legend in my own bathtub? Damn right you are!, I answer quickly and proceed to *cancel the world!* Cheeze! It took the pressure right off the cooker! Sign nothing, sez I! No commitments except to my wife and her belly, plus my own body and soul. FUCKIN KOSMIK! I haven't toilet trained as yet . . . but Gregg only knows, I'm

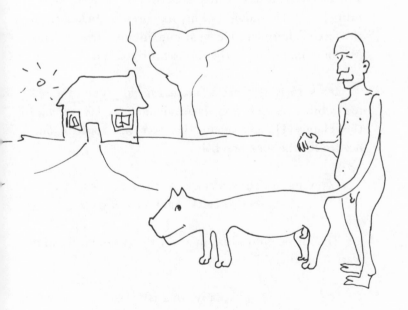

'he was very attached to his dog.'

blissed out on silence et alice, or realizing a potentially *boring decade!*

> THERE'S MORE TO LIFE THAN CRABS
> OR IS THERE?
> KEEP HEALTHY,
> IT'S INTERESTING,
> HI TO SHEILA,
> FUCKMINSTER BULLER,
> A.K.A.
> COUSIN LAWKES.

P.S. lovey dovey

What an inspiration! Ben felt positively fourth street! His cousin's words flooded the canyons of his mime. . . . He thought of his six crises, and laughed in the face of infirmity. He went out singing "Jesus Wants Me for a Sunbeam" at the top of his rigoletto.

It's surprising what a fanatic can do. When the red red robin goes bob bob dylan along. . . . He felt like the Happy Hooker again. He wet his appetite and headed for the sock hop ball.

> One two three a clock four a clock cock
> Five six seven a clock eight a clock cock

The music got to him in a way that would leave him scarred for life.

> (mentally, that is)

CHAPTER FORTY-ONE:

"A COMPLETE CHANGE OF PACEMAKER"

A romantic, suspicious novelty set on the erotic island of Mazurka. Some of the most important characters in the scenario of a grand hotel are to be found behind the bathroom door.

PRISCILLY Ward, for example. To

Priscilly, cleaning a hotel manager isn't a job. It's a way of life. A profession. Like all the chambermaids at the Colonnade Hotel, Priscilly doesn't just tidy up your room; she tidies it *down*. She cleans herself. She believes scrubbing isn't scrubbing unless it's done with a *scrubber*. Like in the old country. *Wherever* that is.

If you think Priscilly's approach too teutonic and water, look at the gender side of it. The way she turns down your head in the evening and lovingly fluffs up her pillow. The way she arranges freshly-cut fingers in your room; the way she proudly leaves a personal calling card on the floor wishing you a pleasant stay. The next time *you* want to stay in a bland hotel, save yourself a trans-Atlantic phone call: Stay with Priscilly, or any other member of our personnel at the Colonnade Hotel.

You will remember in the previous episode that, for over twenty years, Gaga Lang has been haunted by the

question of whether her mother jumped to her death bed
. . . or whether she was discouraged. Only one person
might know—Gaga's partly going, jet-sitting grandmother, Stymie, who lives with her fresh young lover on
Mazurka, in the same house where Gaga's mother fried.

When Gaga writes to her grandmother, she receives
a cable car in reply: Stymie is ill and needs her health.
Alarmed, Gaga gets a rush to Mazurka. But it is too
soon. . . . Her grandmother is deadly. Then in that
strange, fateful house, terriflying things begin to happen. Gaga hears the sound of a baby flying; she thinks
she sees a light gray hound bus. As she is being drawn
carefully, deeper and deeper toward bond and the secret
of her mother's death, she must fight her sanitation department as well as her wife!

The news is broadcast in several languages at once.
Clouds are framed in hardwood. A large pair of black
performers vacuum the manicured lawn of a distinct relative singing in unicorn:

> Well into the distant knight
> Our fathers hung around,
> Looking for the Unholy Alliance
> And digging in the ground.
> The sound of waterbuffalo drilling . . .
> Twas ever thus and more besides.
> The ancient curfew squirms
> (Instead of counting blessings
> They counted suicides).

The sound of Thais dripping . . .
Mustachioed and ruby-lipped;
Twelve salty sailors dance
Whilst leaning to the left a bit
And coming in their pants.
The sound of babies flying . . .
They spruced themselves with oil of chic,
The incense burned their eyes,
And whilst they turned the other cheek
Mosquitos bit their thighs.
The sound of muscles blaspheming . . .
Their search has taken them afar.
Cry out the new unknown!
The size of Turks in Zanzibar
Had drawn them far from home.
The sound of mice slipping . . .
To each his own! Keep off the grass!
The foreign parts decline.
They bent beneath the Khyber Pass
To stitch themselves in time.
The sound of silence bending . . .
All's well that ends well!
The ancient sages spake.
They dig inside Picasso
But find another fake.
The sound of money changing . . .
A sage who knows his onions
Israeli understood.
He robs the dumb to pay the blind,
A kind and Robbing Hood.
The sound of music fainting . . .
Swallow this and preserve your sanity.

I reach in my pocket for another dose of malaria. I search for tomorrow on channel two. A heterosaxophone blows me in the dark; the sweet nymph paints herself into a corner; I kiss her on the lymphs and ask for tea and simplethings, hoping to dog she's paid her dues. I cry in my sleep, perchance to drool.

A vision glides through the door wearing only glad tidings. I listen closely. . . . A friend in knee socks cannot be taken daily. A gray-haired architect gets stoned in a town house. Bad news is to be taken with a pinch of salt. I hold her in my arms, whispering sweet nothanks in her ear.

"My little baby carriage," I said, with an eye to the future. "Please cry quietly; these walls are as cold as ice." A dancing table lamp caught me off guard; I turn over a new leaf and bounce into infinity. . . .

Grandmother enters the room in traditional tweed. She ticks off the old man with a riding crop. The three of them sit on a bed, she knitting, the man fishing for compliments of the season. A typical.

Someone is carrying a large goose across a field followed by an Irish settler. The wine flows freely; the children gaze in awe shucks. The pigs are fed gladly by an out-of-work daughter of the revolution. There's going

to be a picnic! The table is waylaid. Two people are kissing/A hen is tasting the soup. The whole family circle. Everyone is happy. Even the dog has a seat at their table. Such friendliness! A TV guide to the future.

You will stop smoking on July tenth. The will of Allah will be read aloud. If that doesn't work, try Jack LaLanne.

On the horizon, a car zooms in; on its roof, a lonely cow is strapped, legs askew in the air. "On the way to market, no doubt," comments Hannah. A man of letters

exhibitionist!.

delivers the mail; he laughs at the sight of the happy family beneath the old oak tree. They breed like rabbits.

A boy is caught with his pants down and is forgiven. Everyone gets to swing Grandfather from the tree. They wear funny clothes to a mock turtle wedding.

Daddy stalks Stella by sunlight. He licks her into hysterics in the attic. In the evening, less of them eat inside.

Suddenly, the lights fail; Granny gets some candles and all is well again. Only Dorothy is different; she has beheaded herself in shame and discomfort on the cellar floor.

"I *told* you she'd lose her head someday! I knew it all along the watchtower," said a subdued Gramdame. "But still, it could have been worse. She could have lost her *virginian*."

≪ ≫

The old pond
the sound of frog
the smell of Haiku.

The scene is changed far into the maddening crowd. Beggars are singing the praises of one Alice Lipservice.

"Praise be to Alice!" the cry goes up, catching the crowd from behind. "Praise be to Alice! Lightning strikes twice!" And sure enough, two more fell in a sudden death play-off. A long fade panning backward down a tree-lined country lane . . . Grandmother and

Grandfather, waving good riddance to the rain. . . . A
song is heard over their credits . . .

> Don't wave your eyes at me
> Don't shave your legs for me
> Don't talk to the enemy . . .
> People will say we're insane!
> Don't pave the way too much
> Don't show them too much crutch
> Don't talk to the double dutch . . .
> People will say we're in pain!

NEVER UNDERESTIMATE
THE POWER OF
ATTORNEY

ANTONY Newlywed picks up the pieces.

"Hello? Who is speaking French? Speed up; I can't bear you! Speed up, I say; I haven't got Aldo Ray! What's that? You're interested in delivering bicycles? No? Oh, *babies!* No, I don't need any right now. . . . Could you talk behind my back in October? You can? Oh, wonderful! Do I know any people? Of course . . . some of my best friends are people! By the way, what's your name again? I didn't catch it. . . . I will what? I see. . . . Do you take bribes? All right then, *now* you're *talking!* It's just an expression. . . . I know you've been talking . . . Well fuck you, too. . . .

"Who the hell do you think you are? *I know who I am.* . . . I'm Antony Newlywed and I'm picking up the pieces on Atlantic . . . Yes, I've heard of Boris Day . . . the one with dogs . . . It doesn't do a thing for me. . . . Oh, you're Boris Day. . . . Well, why didn't you say so in the first race . . . oh, never mind the formalities . . . I'll do what I can. . . . Really, I don't *need* any

more Alpo. O.K., just a little then, thank you, goodbye."

"You'll never guess in a month of sunstroke who was
on the phone just now," Antony addressed his wife in
silk. "I bet it was Boris Day," said the wife knowingly.
"A-fuckin-mazing, I don't know how you do it," he said
admiringly.

Back to back, they fazed each other out of the script.
The picture was fading through lack of lackeys. A low
budget porno flick involving a pair of crazed nuns and
an anteater; doomed from the start by an up-and-coming
Discreet Attorney who addressed himself to the problem:
"If I can't have it, nobody gets it, O.K.?" He was short
and to the point of no return.

"Level with me, Sol, or pay the fine."

"I will try, Kathy, or my name isn't in the Yellow
Pages." He stands up to greet her on the forehead. "I
want a straight answer, Sol. I'm not one of your two-by-
fours."

"Don't I know that? Don't I know it better than
most? I'm not trying to pull the wool out of your eyes;
I'm deeply concerned with your permission." He clasps
his hands behind his head, eyebrows narrowed in an
attempt to see through her. "I promised I would divorce
her as soon as she gets out of hand."

"You've been handing me that story since you first
got me in the sack, Sol. And I ain't about to buy it no
more. . . . You understand what I'm saying. . . . You
know where I'm coming from?" He knew very well

where she was coming from; he paid the rent. "I'm trying to be unreasonable, Ava, but you're not making it very easy for me."

"I've given you the best part of my body for the last six years and you got the balls to come on like a fuckin' commercial for vaginal spray. . . . Just let me get me 'ands on ya and you won't be asking for a refill for the rest of ya cockridden life, ya grease-covered shithouse." He turned pale, and reached for his wallet.

A few hours later, on Fifth Avenue to be exact, the body of a used astronaut is found face down in a pile of distinction. These two unrelated incidents are later to play a large part in a movie. A hermit crab comes out of hiding to tell his side of the story:

You see, it was like this. Two people desperately in need of medical attention began to auction off each other's belongings. At first, they were as happy as Larry Olivier, if I may be so bold; like two pigs in a riot they were. But later he began to get superstitious, jealous, you know; anyway, it was driving her daisy.

Like I said, he began to have her followed by Alfred Hitchcock. . . . It became like a nightmare for her. How would you like it? She wasn't even safe in her own arms.

I'll never forget the day she caught him napping in a wastepaper basket outside her office window. Thirty floors up . . . He must've been completely mad, now I come to think of it, and I try not to.

Anyway, as I was saying, his face was getting more and more disturbing; he began to resemble Robert Redford in the most peculiar way. . . . I can still see him hanging by the skin of his secretary over the Manhattan skyline . . . and waving to the crowd that had gathered to watch the rescue. How it turned out, I'll never know. . . . I just couldn't look.

The investigation went on four years, each party accusing the other of wider and wider jeans. Simply everyone was wearing them.

Cut to a fur-lined avenue, somewhere on the East Side. Leonardo Bernstein is conducting The New York Donkeys on a tour of duty. A TV diner chases him into the East River. The press are there to hear his statement. "Wet," says Leonardo, vanishing up a wave of his baton rouge. "Remarkable," say the united press and continue to write each other up.

A good time was had by all.

Except for Spencer Tracy, who wasn't all there.

AFTERWORD

THE FIRST TIME I read John's writing was at a book shop in London. I'd gone there to see if they'd stocked my book *Grapefruit*, and I sighed in relief when I found it. Then I noticed John's book. We were on the same shelf, close to each other: John was under *L*; I was under *O*. I flipped through the pages and read "I Sat Belonely." Next I noticed a drawing of an ugly woman whose naked body was covered with flies. God, that was like my film idea!

We'd met briefly at the Indica Gallery; what I remembered most about John from that encounter was that he moved his nose extremely well when I told him to breathe—as part of my artwork. But the book showed me John's soul, a witty, funny, and relentlessly romantic spirit with a taste for the grotesque as well. I never thought for a moment that this was the man I was to share tears and laughter with for many years to come.

John wrote very quickly. Words flowed from his pen like sparkling spring water; he never had to stop to think. In the next decade or so I became immensely spoiled. He would write me little notes and long letters; I would find them in a book I was reading, or on the kitchen table, or next to my toothbrush—something to make me laugh, something to make me feel good, or bad, depending on his mood at the time. And it wasn't just to me. He would pour out his witticisms on paper, even to the lawyers, accountants, and critics who usually upset him.

John wrote *Skywriting* at a time when the world was wondering whatever had happened to him. Why wasn't he writing songs anymore? Well, this was what he was busy doing. He would write one page and ask me to read it back to him, and we'd laugh. It was a fun time. John was very happy with *Skywriting* and proud to share it with me. He thought it was a cinch for a film—but then, all John's writings had a vividly cinematic quality about them. Only their whirlwind spatial changes kept them from being easily realized as films. But that's also what makes John's work very special: he takes us through a thousand sunrises in one page.

I'm glad that I can now share these writings with you. I'm sure John would be, too.

Yoko Ono
February 1986